CU00967555

System of Bible doctrine

To
Jim
from
JACKIE + MARIA
CHRISTMAS 2006

System of
Bible doctrine

John Thornbury

EVANGELICAL PRESS

EVANGELICAL PRESS
Faverdale North Industrial Estate, Darlington, DL3 0PH,
England

Evangelical Press USA
P. O. Box 825, Webster, New York 14580, USA

e-mail: sales@evangelicalpress.org
web: www.evangelicalpress.org

© Evangelical Press 2003. All rights reserved. No part of this
publication may be reproduced, stored in a retrieval system
or transmitted, in any form, or by any means, electronic,
mechanical, photocopying, recording or otherwise, without
the prior permission of the publishers.

First published 2003

**British Library Cataloguing in Publication Data
available**

ISBN 0 85234 526 7

All Scripture quotations, unless otherwise indicated, are taken
from the New King James Version. Copyright © 1982 by
Thomas Nelson, Inc. Used by permission. All rights reserved.

Printed and bound in Great Britain by Creative Print and
Design Wales, Ebbw Vale, South Wales.

Contents

Foreword

There is a great split in theological education today between systematic theology and biblical exegesis. This bifurcation has been brought about in part by increased specialization so that expert scholars know more and more about less and less. On the one hand, biblical scholars labour hard to protect their textual turf from 'those theologians'. At the same time, theologians are tempted to do their work quite detached from dependence upon, and accountability to, what the Holy Scriptures actually teach. It is not necessarily wrong, of course, for contemporary theologians to be informed by philosophical constructs, cultural analysis and literary trends. But what about 'Thus saith the Lord'?

In this volume John Thornbury presents a 'system of Bible doctrine'. Each word is important here. Biblical theology is 'systematic' in that it hangs together. It makes sense as part of an overarching storyline that begins with God's eternal purposes in Christ and will conclude only when God declares that 'time shall be no more'. Despite the incredible diversity within the Bible itself, Holy Scripture has been delivered to us as one single canon of inspired writings. The early Christians interpreted the Old Testament in the light of Jesus Christ, and so must we. The system John Thornbury uses is not an alien philosophical idea imposed upon the biblical text, but rather a principle of orderly presentation that arises from the Bible text itself. Throughout the history of the church, many heresies have arisen precisely because only one aspect of biblical truth has been emphasized at the expense of others. Listening to the whole Bible as an interconnected and unified revelation from God will help us to avoid dangerous lapses from the rule of faith.

This is a system of 'Bible' doctrine in that it assumes that the written Word of God is our only rule for faith and practice in the life of the church. John Stott has said that evangelicals are Bible people and gospel people. These two — Bible and gospel — belong together and should not be pitted against one another. In this theological handbook, John Thornbury is concerned to show what the Bible actually teaches about the things of God and how they relate to the human situation. Many so-called higher critical studies of the Bible are spun out with no reference to the fact that the Bible is the book of the church. Such studies frequently show little if any interest in catechesis, worship, outreach, or spirituality. Nearly a century ago, Karl Barth declared that the purpose of serious Scripture study was not to make the Bible 'relevant' to our modern world, but rather to come to see how irrelevant the modern world — and we ourselves — have become in our rebellion against God. Only a reverent, believing scholarship, one which accepts without apology the total truthfulness of Holy Scripture, can point the church towards such an engagement with God's written Word.

This is a system of Bible 'doctrine'. The very word 'doctrine', like its cousins 'dogma' and 'dogmatic', has fallen on hard times in recent years. For many people it connotes authoritarianism, intellectualism and legalism. Yet despite these misconceptions, the recovery of doctrinal teaching and preaching based on sound biblical theology is essential to the renewal of the church. More and more the world is asking: What does the church have to say that no one else can say?

What does the preacher have to say that the psychologist, politician, stockbroker, or social commentator has not already said with more passion and insight than most pastors can muster even on Easter Sunday? The credibility of the church's proclamation demands biblical tough-mindedness and theological substance.

Doctrine, of course, is not an abstract formulation of belief divorced from the saving reality of God in Jesus Christ. To the contrary, it is the irreducible content of this very reality, conveyed through God's authoritative, infallible Word and elucidated through what the church of Jesus Christ believes, teaches and confesses on the basis of that Holy Word. When doctrine is understood in this holistic, that is to say, salvational-redemptive sense, it will not be seen as ideas to be batted around by ivory-tower theologians, but rather as the stuff of Christian living, the indispensable sinews of sanctification in the life of the believer.

In this book, John Thornbury gives us an example of what I take to be the best definition of theology I have ever heard. This definition was coined by William Ames, a great puritan theologian, whose *Marrow of sacred divinity* was the first textbook of theology adopted by Harvard College when it was founded in 1636. *Theologia est scientia vivendo deo*, 'Theology is the science of living in the presence of the living God.'

Timothy George
(Dean of Beeson Divinity School of Samford University and executive editor of Christianity today*)*

Introduction

The purpose of this little book is to give, in a short, concise and simple way, the main doctrines of the Christian faith as I understand them. It is profound enough, I believe, to benefit scholars and ministers but also elementary enough so that lay people can grasp it.

For too long it has been assumed that the study of doctrine is the business of trained theologians and professional academicians. Many believers are admittedly intimidated by complicated and obscure terms, as well as turned off by concepts which bear the names of scholars, both orthodox and heretical, who have long been dead.

There is widespread belief that the role of a pastor is simply to provide emotional care for the flock and do all he can to enlist them, motivate them and cajole them, but that teaching doctrine is a throwback to horse and buggy days. Yet this attitude is being re-evaluated. Too many evangelical churches are being decimated by inroads of cultists. Others are so desperate to be relevant that they are captive to the latest cultural gimmicks. As a result we are seeing a terrible spiritual bankruptcy in the church.

I have found that when doctrine (meaning teaching) is presented plainly and with good application to real Christians they love it. I have used the truths contained in this book, presented in much the same way as set forth here, in Sunday school classes, mid-week meetings, and even on the radio, as well as in the pulpit. I have also had the privilege of teaching them to college students as well as in the Yalta Bible Institute in the Crimea. Many have expressed deep appreciation for solid preaching and teaching and I am glad to say that our own church, Winfield Baptist of Winfield, Pennsylvania, has developed into a congregation with much relish for the truth.

I have chosen to use few quotations. This is not because I have little regard for the writings of other men and women. I have benefited greatly from our great teachers of the past and present. But this is a study of *Bible doctrine*. My design is to present this material as briefly as possible. Suffice it to say that the doctrines taught here are within the great Calvinistic, evangelical, Baptist stream which is my own heritage. I do not apologize for it.

May all of us take to heart the admonition of Paul: 'Test all things; hold fast what is good' (1 Thess. 5:21).

1.
Learning about God and creation

There are two ways to approach the study of biblical truth: *exegetically* and *theologically*. The exegetical approach is to proceed to investigate the Scriptures book by book, chapter by chapter, verse by verse. This is the best way and the first we should use. After we have done this we can proceed to study the Bible and theology topically, seeking to organize the teachings of the Bible into a *system of truth*. Just as the universe is the 'material for investigation' for the secular scientist (geologists, astronomers, etc.), so the Bible is the source for the theologian. To be without a *system* of theology is to live in spiritual confusion.

Concepts of God

Is there a God? If so, what is he like? This question has fascinated peoples of all ages and cultures from the beginning of recorded history. It would be safe to say that the religious instinct is one of the most powerful inclinations of human nature. An ancient Greek writer once pointed out that no community has been found where there is not some form of worship and religion.

Of course the big question is: 'What is God like?' First, let us look at some of the major concepts of God.

The materialistic view

This is essentially atheism. This view propounds the concept that matter is self-sufficient and eternal: the source and end of all things. Carl Sagan once said, 'The Universe is all there is.'[1] This view holds that order, life, sensation, instinct, reason, conscience, etc. are all the products of lifeless atoms.

The polytheistic view

Most of the ancient peoples believed that there are many gods, although some of them held that there is one supreme god among the many. The ancient Greeks, who were one of the most advanced and civilized of all peoples, had, in addition to the supreme god Zeus, a god of culture: Apollo; a god of music: Orpheus; a god of love: Aphrodite; a god of war: Ares, etc.

The pantheistic view

Pantheism is the belief that God is all things and all things are in God. A modified view of this is seen in the native Americans. They looked upon earth as the 'mother' of all things and worshipped 'her'. This view has been revived somewhat in the 'New Age' movement, which is aided and abetted by the extreme environmentalists who look upon the earth as the source of our life.

Theism

This is the view that there is a personal God. There are many different concepts of theism, of course. A deist would believe that there is a personal God but he is not directly involved in the affairs of this world. But the God of Judeo-Christianity is redemptive, and people on earth can have a personal relationship to him. In our study we will emphasize this view.

Reasons for believing in a personal God

Are there logical or rational (according to reason) arguments for believing in a personal God? Suppose we do not have a Bible and are thrown into the world with nothing but our own minds and the universe around us. Can we come to the conclusion that there is a God? Would there be proof of a supreme God?

Many arguments have been presented to prove the existence of God. Some of these arguments are difficult to follow and prove not the existence of God but the existence of theologians. Some arguments are inconclusive. The following concepts are plain and simple and have convinced most people that there is a God.

The argument from cause and effect

A fundamental principle of thought, accepted by most people (some deny it but in actual practice act as if it were so), is that every effect must have an adequate cause. The greater the effect the greater the cause must have been. For example, a pair of spectacles could not have just happened. They had to be designed by someone. The spectacles are the effect; the designers and manufacturers are the cause. A computer is a much more complex and intricate device, and it too must have a cause. The sophistication necessary to design and manufacture a computer is far more than that which designed the spectacles, but in both cases the object was produced or 'caused'. As far as our experience is

concerned (we have no other basis of judgement), physical
and mechanical objects are designed and produced.

Now look at the universe. It is immense and very complex. The solar system is an amazing arrangement of planets
orbiting around one large thermonuclear ball that is over
800,000 miles wide and is called the sun. Centrifugal force
and gravity keep the planets in orbit. One of these planets,
the earth, is the exact distance from the sun to have sufficient heat to give life, but not so much as to scorch organisms on it. Was all this by accident? Theists say no. It had to
be designed by an infinitely wise and powerful God. This is
called the cosmological argument.

The ethical argument

It is true that many people argue that they do not believe
that there are absolute rights and wrongs. Some say that
right is what people make it to be. For example, here in our
culture we say it is wrong to kill, and for us it *is* wrong. But
if a community decided that murder is legitimate, then there
would be nothing wrong with it. But deep down, in their
unguarded moments, people reveal that they have a
consciousness that there is a *fitness in things*, which goes
beyond community standards.

If we admit that there is an absolute standard of right
and wrong, as the human conscience seems to teach, then
we must ask who made these laws and who can enforce
them. If it is inherently right that we do not take someone
else's property or life, then we are saying that there is an
absolute law above and beyond us. But if there is no supreme
God to enforce these laws, then they are meaningless. The
fact is that the human conscience, as distorted as it is at
times, reflects the reality of some Higher Power, who gave
the law and will carry out its demands.

The teleological argument

Both of the above arguments for the existence of God are confirmed by the consideration that without belief in a personal God life and history are meaningless and have no direction. What is the meaning of life? Where is history going? Does the individual have significance, and if so, why? Will things turn out all right in the end? Certainly we could take the position that the whole world will eventually explode and all life will be exterminated, just as it came into existence: through (as some would affirm) an accidental explosion. But most people can see that there does seem to be direction to history. Real progress is made. Problems are solved. Why is this? Is it not more reasonable to believe that a great and powerful hand is directing history to some definite conclusion? This line of reasoning is called the *teleological* argument.

Logical processes of the mind and the human conscience induce us to come to the conclusion that there is a supreme God. Certainly in highly developed and civilized societies the belief in a 'Higher Power' is very pervasive. The over-whelming majority of people in such countries as Great Britain and the United States acknowledge the existence of God. Certainly polytheism and atheism are far from dead, but theism historically seems to be winning the ideological battle. We believe the existence of God is a 'first truth', a presupposition which is at the foundation of all knowledge.

Why does not God prove that he exists?

Many people might raise the question of why, if God exists, he does not settle the issue once and for all and come down and boldly show himself to the whole world? Actually the Bible begins with the assumption of God, with the words,

'In the beginning God'. God does not seem overly concerned about defending his existence. In answer to this question we might say two things. First, we believe that God has written his name in the universe very clearly through the physical creation and this should be proof enough. His infinite wisdom is seen in every star and even in every leaf and insect. Secondly, God will eventually do just what the objector demands. Some day God will send his Son visibly and will hold court justifying the righteous and judging the wicked. Then none will be able to gainsay his reality.

Characteristics of God

God is far greater than we can ever conceive him to be, and is greater than any verbal expressions about him. He is infinite and in some respects inscrutable (cannot be fully comprehended or investigated), but we can know much about him. The following classifications are fundamental. They denote characteristics, or attributes, of God.

Unity

God exists as a single essence of substance. He is one and there is no being of the same nature (Deut. 6:4; 2 Sam. 7:22; Ps. 86:10; Isa. 43:10; 1 Cor. 8:6; Gal. 3:20; 1 Tim. 2:5). Human reason confirms the fact of the unity of God. More than one supreme being is inconceivable. There could be many great and powerful beings, but only one could be supreme.

Personality

God is a being who knows, feels, wills and speaks, etc. This is so evident from the Bible that no proof text is required.

All the attributes of personality are ascribed to God. Some people speak of 'God' in a vague way, meaning some influence that pervades all things, but is not personal. This differs from the God of Scripture.

Eternity

God's existence is without beginning or end (Gen. 21:33; Ps. 90:2; Isa. 40:28). Is God timeless? See 2 Peter 3:8. The name of *Yahweh*, the Hebrew God, means 'I am'. Jesus appropriated this term for himself (John 8:58). The Bible speaks of God as relating to history, the present and the future; but human faculties are unable to conceive of existence apart from time. God is not limited in any way by it.

Spirituality

God is a pure spirit (John 4:24; Ps. 139:7). He has no physical shape or what is called 'corporeality', that is, body or bodily parts. Matter, or the material universe, requires space due to its very nature. But spirit does not. Since God is an infinite Spirit, he fills all space. The Bible speaks of the eyes, ears, hands of the Lord, etc., but these are mere symbols of his activity, and are not to be taken literally.

Independence

God is above all his creatures in all he is and does. He is independent in his existence. He has life in himself. He has independent knowledge (John 2:24-25; Heb. 4:13). He is independent in actions (Dan. 4:25, 35; Eph. 1:11). God is absolutely sovereign and has the right to do anything he wishes. He is independent in happiness (Acts 17:24-25). He is pleased with the obedience of men and angels, but his happiness does not depend upon a relationship with other

intelligent beings. He was infinitely happy and blessed before there were any creatures.

Immutability

God is forever the same in knowledge, character, purpose
and blessedness (Mal. 3:6; Ps. 102:27; Heb. 1:12; 13:8; James
1:17). He cannot change for the better because he is already
perfect; nor can he change for the worse for then he would
cease to be perfect. Although God appears to change to us,
and is represented in Scripture as repenting (Gen. 6:7), this
only means that he is 'grieved at heart', not that he mutates.

Omniscience

God knows everything. He knows all things and events that
ever have been or ever will be, either actual or possible. His
understanding is infinite (1 Kings 8:39; Ps. 147:5; Isa. 42:9;
Jer. 1:5; Jer. 16:17; John 2:24). God also knows all the
thoughts of men. He knows the end from the beginning,
thus he has foreknowledge (Isa. 46:10).

Omnipresence

God is represented in Scripture as filling the universe, but he is
also present at every individual point and place (1 Kings 8:27;
Ps. 139:7-12; Jer. 23:23-24; Matt. 18:20). This is because of
his spiritual nature. God cannot be multiplied or divided;
this means that in his total essence he fills the universe.

Omnipotence

God has all power. He can do anything that is consistent
with his own nature or anything that is in harmony with

the laws of truth he has established (Ps. 115:3; Matt. 19:26; Eph. 1:19). Genesis 18:14 says that nothing is too hard for the Lord. When the Bible says that God 'cannot' lie (Titus 1:2), it means that it is against his nature to do so. All the mighty acts of God, such as creation, salvation or raising the dead, show that he can do anything.

Love

God desires the welfare of men, in fact, of all his creatures (Ps. 145:8-9; Matt. 5:44-48). It is the nature of God to do good to his creatures and bestow blessings upon them. We need, however, to distinguish several aspects of the love of God. There is God's compassion upon men generally (John 3:16). There is the sovereign and discriminating love he has to the elect in an unsaved state (Rom. 9:13). There is God's delight in those who love him (Prov. 8:17). God's grace is his unmerited favour towards the guilty. He shows his mercy by withholding justice from those who deserve punishment. He is patient in forbearing to exercise his wrath upon sinners. Other words in Scripture which describe aspects of God's gracious nature are kindness, goodness, pity, etc.

Righteousness

God's moral nature is just and righteous, and is the source of moral law to all created intelligent beings (Lev. 19:2; Deut. 32:4; Ps. 11:7; Ps. 33:5; Hab. 1:13; Rev. 4:8). God cannot conceive or do wrong. Everything he does is right, even though we do not always understand his way. God is himself the standard, and he is always self-consistent. It is possible that God's holiness is simply his self-consistence.

Even though we have listed this attribute towards the end, this characteristic of God is his primary and essential

attribute as far as his relationship to moral agents is concerned. God must be holy; he cannot be otherwise.

The justice of God is God's holiness or righteousness as it
relates to his government of the world. God must punish
sin because he is holy.

Tri-unity

God is one in substance but there are distinctions in the
nature of God that must be recognized. This point will now
be considered separately.

The Trinity

A. H. Strong, the Baptist theologian, said, 'In the nature of
the one God there are three eternal distinctions which are
represented to us under the figure of persons, and these three
are equal.'[2] This statement involves great mystery. Many
would say that it is a puzzle. Yet this defines the orthodox
doctrine of the Trinity held by historic Christianity and it is
taught in the Bible. In considering the fact of the Trinity,
the following points should be considered.

There are distinctions in the Godhead

1. The distinction Father, Son and Holy Spirit *occurs in the
   same context* (Matt. 28:19; 2 Cor. 13:14).
2. The distinctions are *eternal.* The Scriptures assert the
   eternity of the Holy Spirit and the Son (John 1:1-2; Heb.
   9:14).
3. The three distinctions are *represented to us as persons,*
   although there is no division of nature or essence. The
   following points seem to justify the use of the word
   'person' with reference to the distinctions in the Trinity.

a. Personal acts are ascribed to them. The Father begets, the Son is begotten (John 3:16; 1 John 5:1). The Father sends, the Son is sent (1 John 4:9; 4:14).
b. Personal pronouns are used.
c. They communicate with each other (Ps. 110:1; John 17:5).
4. They are *equal*. This will be seen in the following points.

Each of the persons is God

1. *The Father is recognized as God* (John 6:27; 1 Peter 1:2).
2. *The Son is recognized as God.*
   a. He is called God (John 1:1; Rom. 9:5; Titus 2:13; Heb. 1:8; 1 John 5:20). (Christians should have these verses to hand when witnessing to Jehovah's Witnesses.)
   b. Old Testament passages referring to God are applied to the Son (Isa. 40:3; Matt. 3:3).
   c. He possesses the attributes of God: eternity (John 1:1), omnipresence (Matt. 28:20; Eph. 1:23; John 3:13), omniscience (Matt. 9:4; John 2:24-25; John 16:30; 1 Cor. 4:5; Col. 2:3), omnipotence (Matt. 28:18; Rev. 1:8), self-existence (John 5:26), immutability (Heb. 13:8).
   d. The works of God are ascribed to him: creation (John 1:3; 1 Cor. 8:6; Col. 1:16), preservation of the universe (Col. 1:17; Heb. 1:3), raising the dead and judgement (John 5:27-28; Matt. 25:31-32).
   e. He receives the honour and worship due to God alone (John 5:23; Heb. 1:6; 2 Peter 3:18; 2 Tim. 4:18).
3. *The Holy Spirit is recognized as God.*
   a. He has God's attributes: eternity (Heb. 9:14), omniscience (1 Cor. 2:10), omnipresence (Ps. 139:7).
   b. He is represented as doing the works of God: creation (Gen. 1:2; Ps. 33:6), regeneration (John 3:8; Titus 3:5), resurrection (Rom. 8:11).

  c. Father, Son and Holy Spirit are associated together
     on equal footing in the baptism formula (Matt. 28:19)
     and in the apostolic benediction (2 Cor. 13:14).

Creation

The meaning of creation

'Creation' is sometimes used in the sense of a work of art or
genius. For example, the guide in an art gallery might say,
'The work you see on the left is the creation of Picasso.' But
in the biblical sense creation means the production or bringing into existence of something out of nothing.

The fact of creation

The Bible abounds in statements that all of the universe
comes from God's creative power (Gen. 1:1; Ps. 33:6, 9; Ps.
148:5-6; Isa. 40:26; 42:5; Mal. 2:10; Heb. 11:3).

God's motive in creation

Why did God create a universe? We must understand that
creation was not a necessity as far as God is concerned but
a result of his own deliberate, rational choice.

  The Scriptures reveal very clearly that God created the
universe to be a theatre to display his own glory (Prov. 16:4;
Isa. 43:7; Rom. 11:36; Col. 1:16; Rev. 4:11).

  This does not rule out the fact that God had something
else in mind and that is to make intelligent creatures upon
whom he could bestow his blessings. In the history of God's
dealings with people since creation he has showered blessings
upon both angels and men. We must conclude that doing

good to his creatures was also one of God's motives (Ps. 145:9).

God's method in creation

1. *By fiat.* Fiat means 'done by a command'. God spoke the universe into existence (Ps. 33:6; Heb. 11:3).
2. *Without previously existing material* (Heb. 11:3). Some modern scientists explain the universe by a 'big bang', which started when a cosmic egg exploded. But where did the egg come from? Why did it explode? The Scriptures teach that God did not produce the universe from an egg, but out of nothing.
3. *Through Jesus Christ.* The Bible represents all God's works as coming through the purpose of the Father, the authority of the Son, and the agency of the Holy Spirit. In creation, inspiration and redemption God the Father is the Architect, the Son is the Administrator, and the Spirit is the Constructor. Jesus Christ is the divine authoritative source through which all God's creative acts are performed (John 1:3, 10; Col. 1:16; Heb. 1:2-3).

The order of creation

The first chapter of Genesis lays out God's method in making the universe.

1. *The 'raw material' stage.* Genesis 1:1 tells us that in the beginning God created the heavens and the earth. Following this it says that the earth was at first 'without form and void'. This evidently means that the raw material from which the earth came (which was itself created by God) was an inchoate and formless mass. It is possible that this preceded the seven-day period mentioned later.

2. *The separation stage.* On the first day the light and the darkness were divided (v. 5). On the second day the cloudy vapour was separated from the earth (vv. 7-8). Then on the third day the land was separated from the sea (v. 9).

3. *The plant life stage.* The flora or plant life appeared on the third day (vv. 11-13).

4. *The heavenly bodies stage.* These appeared on the fourth day (vv. 14-19). Verse 16 states that God 'made' two great lights. This is not the same word as the one that is translated 'create' in verse 1. The word for 'made' here is *'asah'*. The word for create is *'bara'*. *Bara* seems to refer to bringing into existence something out of nothing. But 'made' or *asah* could imply simply that the lights appeared on the fourth day. There was already light before the fourth day (v. 4). If this light was from the sun, then the sun would have already existed but simply appeared on the fourth day.

5. *The sea creatures and birds stage.* These were made on the fifth day (vv. 20-22).

6. *The land creatures stage.* The rest of the fauna (land animals such as cattle) were created on the sixth day, along with man. Notice in verse 26 that God is represented as plural. 'Let *us* make man'. This seems to point to an early representation of the Trinity.

Were the days of Genesis twenty-four-hour periods?

This question is posed because some modern scientists affirm that the universe is billions of years old. How could this be if the world was made in one week and the chronology of Genesis is taken literally? Assuming that the world is very old as some scientists tell us, there have been several ways to harmonize Scripture with this theory.

1. *The 'age-day' theory.* This view states that the days of Genesis were long periods of time. Admittedly 'day' in the Bible sometimes does not refer to a twenty-four-hour period (Isa. 22:5; John 8:56; Heb. 3:8).
2. *The 'vision-day' theory.* This teaches that the days were not the sequence in creation itself but days in the life of Moses who on consecutive days had visions of creation.

   There are strong reasons, however, to believe that the days are literal days in historical sequence. Notice that the days had 'evening and morning' (Gen. 1:8). This points to days ruled by the sun. Also the seventh 'day' is the basis for the weekly Sabbath which was given to Israel (Exod. 20:11).
3. *The gap theory.* This is another view put forth by believers to bring the teachings in the Bible into harmony with the modern scientific view of the extreme antiquity of the earth. It teaches that there was a creation between Genesis 1:1 and 2 which was destroyed. This, supposedly, explains the ancient fossils which would have been a part of a pre-Adamic order. Jeremiah 4:23-26 is used in support of this view.

Angels

The Bible teaches that there are two orders of intelligent beings which have been created by God: angels and men. They are similar in many ways and dissimilar in other ways. One way in which they are similar is that both have been created with intelligence and moral agency, and both are responsible for their actions. They are, in other words, subject to rewards and punishment. The first of the two orders of rational beings which God created are angels. An entire chapter of study will be given to Bible teaching about man, since this concerns us most directly.

The origin of angels

Clearly angels came forth from the creative power of God
(see Ps. 148:2-5 and Col. 1:16).

The characteristics of angels

1. *Spiritual.* The angels are like God in the sense that they
   do not have material form, although they are often visible
   (see Heb. 1:14; Eph. 6:12; and Mark 12:25).
2. *Intelligent.* See 2 Samuel 14:20. When Jesus said 'not
   even the angels' know when he will come, he implied
   that they have great knowledge (Mark 13:32). Angels
   have been with God a long time. Do they learn? Presumably they do, and if so they must know a great deal.
3. *Powerful.* See 2 Peter 2:11. An angel rolled away from the
   tomb a stone that probably weighed several tons (Matt.
   28:2). Angels will separate the wicked from the righteous
   when Jesus returns (Matt. 13:41). Jesus said that 10,000
   angels could have come to protect him (Matt. 26:53).

The number of angels

Daniel 7:10 states that ten thousand times ten thousand
stood before God, which amounts to 100,000,000. That is
how many unfallen angels there are (see also Deut. 33:2;
Ps. 68:17; and Rev. 5:11).

The organization of angels

Jude 9 refers to Michael, the archangel. Gabriel is a great
angel (Luke 1:19). In Matthew 26:53 Jesus refers to legions
of angels. A legion was a division in the Roman army. This
seems to imply that there are ranks of angels.

The evil angels

God is not the author of evil, or of evil beings. All that God created is 'good' (Gen. 1:31). But there are both holy or elect angels (Mark 8:38; 1 Tim. 5:21), and evil angels or demons.

1. *The leader of the hosts of evil.* The leader of the company of fallen angels is Satan, meaning the adversary, or enemy. He is also called 'the devil', meaning the slanderer or false accuser. Symbolic references to Satan are the dragon (Rev. 12:9), serpent (Rev. 12:9), 'angel of light' (2 Cor. 11:14) and lion (1 Peter 5:8).

2. *The origin of evil.* There was a great apostasy in heaven involving a revolt against the supreme God. This is apparently referred to in Ezekiel 28:12-19 and Isaiah 14:12-15, although the passages are addressed to the Kings of Tyre and Babylon respectively. In the Scriptures prophetic and apocalyptic truths are often cast within the context of historical events (see the prophecy of Christ, Isa. 7:14). Revelation 12:7-9 and Jude 6 also discuss the war in heaven and the conflict between Satan and Christ.

3. *The work of evil angels*
   a. Opposing God (Isa. 14:13; Matt. 13:39).
   b. Deceiving man (Rev. 20:3).
   c. Tempting and leading men astray (1 Chron. 21:1; John 13:2, 27).
   d. Blinding and controlling the unsaved (John 8:44; Acts 26:18; 2 Cor. 4:4-5; 2 Tim. 2:26).
   e. Accusing, testing, hindering, resisting and buffeting God's people (Job 1:6, 9; Zech. 3:1; Luke 22:31; 1 Thess. 2:18).

   f. Causing physical disease. The devil causes sickness
      (Luke 13:16; Acts 10:38), and has the power of death
      (Heb. 2:14).

4. *The number of the fallen angels.* Some conclude from
   Revelation 12:4 that one third of the angels are fallen.

The holy or elect angels

1. They worship God (Ps. 103:20; Heb. 1:6).
2. They rejoice in God's works.
   a. Creation (Job 38:4-7).
   b. The salvation of sinners (Luke 15:10).
3. They supervise the affairs of nations (Dan. 10:13; 12:1).
4. They are involved in the interventions of God in history.
   a. Giving of the law (Heb. 2:2).
   b. Prophetic office (Dan. 9:22).
   c. Birth of Christ (Luke 1:26; 2:13-15).
   d. Resurrection of Christ (John 20:12).
   e. Ascension of Christ (Acts 1:9-11).
   f. Judgement (Matt. 13:41-42).
5. They protect and assist individual believers (Ps. 34:7; 1
   Kings 19:5-8; Heb. 1:14).
6. They take interest in divine truth and learn through the
   church (1 Cor. 11:10; Eph. 3:10; 1 Peter 1:12).

The will of God

How does God govern his creatures who are rational, intelligent and responsible? The physical universe is controlled
by physical laws, the animal creation by instinct, etc. The
planetary system operates on principles of gravity and
motion. The life processes of plant life follow well-known
and predictable laws of biology.

But when it comes to angels and men, we have a different situation. They have moral agency, freedom and responsibility and thus cannot be governed by mere physical force. Although human beings are subject to the physical, chemical and biological processes, the realm of the mind is special. The power to choose puts rational beings in a different category than lower forms of life, such as plant life or even the highest forms of animals.

Given that intelligent creatures have freedom and responsibility, does this mean God *never* determines that his own will is enforced in their conduct? God is infinitely more powerful than any created beings and can control them. But if he enforces his will does he make men machines and puppets? These questions involve many problems that we may never fully solve, but we should strive to understand the problem correctly. We should also be sure that we understand what the Bible teaches on this subject. We need to hold sound views on the nature of human psychology and the plan of God. The following distinctions relate to God's will.

His revealed will

Sometimes the will of God refers to *that which God desires,* as indicated by what he commands us to do. We refer to this as his revealed will.

1. The will of God refers to that which is *right in his sight* (see Ezra 7:18; Mark 3:35; Rom. 12:2; Eph. 6:6; 1 Peter 2:15). For example:

a. The Ten Commandments, which were given to Israel (Exod. 20:1-17).
b. God's command for people to repent and believe (Acts 17:30; 1 John 3:23).

2. There are *special situations* in history when God placed upon his people obligations, which were for a limited time only.

a. God commanded Adam and Eve to avoid the tree of the knowledge of good and evil (Gen. 2:17).
b. Israel was given the commandment of circumcision (Gen. 17:10).
c. Baptism and the Lord's Supper are special ordinances peculiar to the church in this age (Matt. 28:19; 1 Cor. 11:23-24).

3. In Scripture the will of God often refers to *God's gracious desires* and good wishes for his creatures. God is merciful and good to men; his thoughts are thoughts of peace. God does not delight in the pains and sufferings of his creatures (see Ezek. 18:23; Luke 13:34; 2 Peter 3:9).

Man's responsibility

The government of the universe cannot be maintained on the basis of God's desire alone. This aspect of God's will, his revealed will or will of desire, addresses specifically man's responsibility. But is this the only aspect of God's will? If it were, we would find ourselves with the following problems:

1. *God could not predict the future.* A parent gives commands and responsibilities to his or her children, but can a parent infallibly predict what course the child will take? No. The community can make laws, but can public officials know in advance how people will relate to them? No. So, if God only has a will of desire as the basis of his commandments to people, then he would not be able to foreknow the future.

2. *Any redemptive plan of God could conceivably fail.* If the only activity of God is to instruct men as to their duty, without moving to accomplish any definite results, his government might fall into chaos and collapse. Possibly no one would ever do the will of God, for it is conceivable that none would choose to obey the Creator.

3. *Righteous people would live in uncertainty, fear and doubt because evil might eventually triumph.* They would be serving a being who either could not or would not ensure that those things he most desires would come about.

But we need not fear such a disaster, for the Bible reveals that there is another aspect to the will of God, a will that cannot be thwarted or frustrated.

God's sovereign will

The will of God has reference to that which God has determined to come about. We refer to this as God's secret or sovereign will, which would include the great works of God for which he is directly responsible. But it also encompasses the sinful acts of men which he permits but overrules for his own glory (see Isa. 46:9-10; Dan. 4:35; Eph. 1:5; Rev. 17:17).

1. *God's determinative decrees.* Some specific examples of works of God, in which his sovereign will is effectual and is determinative, are:

a. Creation (Ps. 148:5; Rev. 4:11)
b. The inspiration of the Bible (2 Peter 1:21)
c. The work of Jesus Christ
  • His coming into the world (Gal. 4:4).
  • His death (Acts 2:23; 1 Peter 1:19).
  • His second coming (Acts 17:31; Heb. 9:28).

d. The salvation of God's people. Throughout Scripture the
   redemption of man is ascribed to God.
   • Predestination unto adoption (Eph. 1:5).
   • Regeneration (John 1:12; James 1:18).
   • The preservation of the saints (Matt. 18:14).
e. The future conversion of Israel (Jer. 31:31-33).

2. *God's providence.* The way God preserves and governs the
world is part of his will or determination. God's providence
is holy, wise and powerful, and embraces everything he has
made, with all their actions. All beings owe their continued
existence, with all their properties and powers, to God (Neh.
9:6; Ps. 104:21; Ps. 148:6-8; Matt. 10:29).

3. *God's permissive decrees.* Is there a sense in which the
sinful acts of angels or men are the will of God? It is not
conceivable that they can be according to the revealed will
of God, as described earlier. But the Bible does attribute
the sinful conduct of responsible beings to God in some
sense.

a. This is true of evil spirits (1 Kings 22:21-22).
b. This is true of evil men (2 Sam. 16:10; 1 Kings 12:15, 24;
   2 Chron. 25:20; Ps. 105:25; Zech. 8:10).

How are we to understand these passages? Since God is
utterly holy and cannot even look upon sin (Hab. 1:13), and
tempts no man (James 1:13), they mean that God by
definite choice determined not to prevent the evil deeds
spoken of and overruled them for his glory. Psalm 76:10
says God makes the wrath of man to praise him and Romans
8:28 teaches that all things are working out for the good of
God's people. When we speak of God permitting sin, we
define this as God's *permissive* will.

Practical questions

1. *The relation of God's foreknowledge and purpose.* The foreknowledge of God is attested to many times in Scripture (Acts 15:18; Acts 2:23; 1 Peter 1:2). This is not mere foresight, for even men can know things that are going to happen in certain circumstances. Daniel foresaw the destruction of the Roman Empire (2:44), because God revealed it to him. These who foresee the future either receive information from an infallible outside source, or they have the ability to bring the foreseen events to pass. Since the first of these options cannot be true of God, the second must be. Therefore foreknowledge is based on predetermination, not vice versa.

2. *God's will and secondary causes.* All God's plans take into account secondary causes and choices of men. God uses means to carry out his purpose. For example, God planned to destroy the city of Jericho, but he used the army of Israel to accomplish this.

3. *The use and abuse of predestination.* God's sovereign plan and providence imply that he has control over all the events of history. This is a glorious truth and is full of comfort to the people of God. But it should never be used to justify wicked acts of negligence of our duty. The truth of sovereignty should be accepted with reverence and taught with prudence and in harmony and balance with the parallel truth of human accountability.

2.
Learning about the Bible

When Sir Walter Scott, the famous British novelist and poet, was on his deathbed, he said to those standing nearby, 'Bring me the book.' 'Which book?' one asked. 'There are many books.' 'Yes,' he replied, 'there are many books, but I want *the* book, the Bible.' Indeed the Bible is *the* book. It is far and away the most widely read book in the history of mankind, and no other piece of literature can compare with it as far as influence is concerned.

A revelation from God is needed

Assuming that there is an eternal, all-powerful God who has created man, it is reasonable to conclude that he would reveal himself to man in some way suitable to him as a rational, intelligent and inquisitive creature. The deepest and most important questions that relate to man's nature, origin and destiny cannot be answered by man with his unaided reason. This is illustrated in a comment made by the well-known stunt cyclist, Evel Knievel, before his famous jump over Snake River Canyon, in Idaho, USA. He said that there are three questions which he could not answer. These are, 'Where did I come from?'; 'Where am I going?'; and 'What am I here for?' These are not trivial questions; they are matters that every reflective person has asked, from the greatest philosophers to the ordinary man in the street.

The stunt cyclist's questions show that we need a revelation from God. Here are some reasons why.

To explain the origin of things

Where can we go to find answers to the questions raised by Evel Knievel? For example, where can we find out about the origin of things? There are many theories about the origin of man and the universe. Science with all its vast resources cannot really give a final answer as to the sources of existence. The concept of evolution takes us back to elementary, primordial organisms which supposedly developed into modern man over a process of millions of years. But this view has been challenged even by many modern non-Christian scientists who claim that there is no real evidence for this view. The enormous 'gaps' in the evolutionary chain still remain a colossal problem for evolutionists. If, as evolutionists say, the various species evolved from simpler forms of life, there should be millions of transitional forms, but there are none.

What about the universe as a whole? Various theories have been propounded, but they are usually short-lived. Models for how the universe began are presented, refuted, discarded, and in a few years largely forgotten. Gerald P. Kuiper, a contemporary American astronomer, has pointed out that all possible theories about the *origin of the solar system* probably involve assumptions that are simply beyond man's power to verify. 'It is not a foregone conclusion,' he asserts, '...that the problem has a scientific solution. For example, an enclosure in which the air has been stirred gives, after some delay, no clue to the nature or the time of the stirring. All memory of the event within the system has been lost.'[3]

Writing on 'The Origin and Evolution of the Universe', Sir Bernard Lovell says, 'Although with our telescopes we shall no doubt clarify the cosmological problem to a large extent, the ultimate issue of the origin of the cosmos may well be a metaphysical one lying outside the realms which the tools of physics and astronomy can approach for reasons which are inherent in fundamental scientific theory.'[4] Such concessions from eminent scientists are quite significant, given the fact that some scientists claim to have ultimate answers in not only science but philosophy and religion.

To explain life after death

Man is incurably inquisitive about the future. In our own day, practitioners in foretelling abound. Mystics, fortune tellers, palm readers and students of astrology have millions of devoted followers. There have always been people who have claimed to be able to peer into the future. But how can anyone be sure that they are right? One well-known prophetess, Jean Dixon, has made many false predictions yet some still place great confidence in her.

The non-Christian religions of the world offer no solution to the problem of the nature and destiny of man. Chaos and confusion characterize the realms of cultic theories. Some believe that man is just an animal and will perish like them. Some believe that mortals are reincarnated into different species at some time following their deaths. From the actual results thus far we can put little confidence in the studies of man about the future. Obviously we need some light from God to show the way.

To explain the meaning of life

What about the nature of man and the purpose of his existence? Since human beings are rational, self-conscious creatures they are always asking themselves, 'Who am I?' Self-identity is a fundamental pursuit of the human personality, but what does this introspection produce in the way of concrete knowledge? A great deal, as far as our physical and psychological make-up is concerned. But what about the spiritual dimensions? Does man have a soul? Again, some super-human authority must speak.

What about goals and purpose in life? Are we to seek no higher end in this world than survival and reproduction? Can we find supreme satisfaction in the pleasures of the mind and the body on this earth? The opportunities of the world may well be fulfilling and significant, yet there are nagging questions in man about the problems of religion. The identity crisis most people feel is not the only difficulty. There is a motivational crisis as well. What is life all about? What should we live for? We need direction from God in these matters.

To explain the nature of God

What about God himself? Many strong reasons point to the existence of a Supreme Being, but what is he like? We can see from the universe that God is a being with great power and wisdom. The glory of a Creator is displayed in everything in the physical universe, from microscopic organisms to the distant stars. But what are his moral attributes? Is he a God of love and grace? Apart from some specific revelation these questions go unanswered.

The Bible claims to be God's revelation

There is a book that purports to answer the basic questions about God and man and their relationship to each other. It is the Bible. It describes in great detail the *beginnings* of the universe and the earth, the origin and nature of man. It reveals a *higher goal* for man than living for time and physical satisfaction. It gives a thorough description of the characteristics of the God who made us. It records the history of the great works and acts of God in the history of the world, and forecasts the future of the earth and its peoples. It gives a satisfying explanation of the causes of the miseries of mankind and shows what God has done to deal with them.

Certain undeniable facts about the Bible

1. *The antiquity of the Bible.* One cannot but be impressed with the fact that the Bible has been appealed to for religious instruction for centuries. Its roots go back to the days of ancient Israel when the Hebrew Scriptures were studied by wise men and prophets. These were combined with the writings of the apostles to form a unity and were handed down from generation to generation during the Christian era. Even in the days of primitive writing methods they have been carefully copied and preserved. In spite of many problems in the Christian community, from within and without, the teachings of the Bible have been carried on. Nations have risen and fallen, philosophical systems have waxed and waned, and great changes have taken place in all realms of human thought and activity, but still the message of the Bible has been preached, believed and practised.

The Bible has survived in spite of innumerable enemies and obstacles. Atheists and infidels have cursed it, inquisitors have burned it, religious authorities have protested vehemently against it, scientists have laughed at it, yet it remains today the world's most studied book.

2. *The influence of the Bible.* The Bible has without question had the most far-reaching impact of any book in the history of mankind. For many years it held the field as the authoritative basis for faith and morals in the western world.

Until the rise of the so-called scientific age it provided the cultural and social framework for the United States, England and much of Europe. Since the rise of the missionary age about two hundred years ago it has been increasingly influential in parts of the Third World, notably Africa, South America and Indonesia. The impact of the Bible has been extensive and varied.

a. *On human government.* The impact of the Bible on government has been great. The American President takes his oath of office with his hand on the Bible. Texts of Scripture are written all over our coins and public buildings.

b. *On art and literature.* Many of the works of the great artists deal with biblical scenes and themes. The works of William Shakespeare, the prince of English authors, abound with quotations from the Bible.

c. *On religion.* The Bible is the basis of faith and living for the most populous religion on earth, Christianity. In 1994 over 1,800,000,000 of the world's people professed to follow Jesus Christ, whose life and ministry are recorded in the Bible. The next most populous religion is Islam, which has about half as many adherents as Christianity.

d. *On the social systems of the world.* The influence of the Bible has been both direct and indirect. Its direct influence has come about through preaching, evangelism and missionary work on the part of the various Christian communities. But the Judeo-Christian way of thinking, based on Scripture, has also produced great social reforms and revolution. The anti-slavery movement, prison reform, and many of the great benevolent and philanthropic movements have been inspired and rooted in biblical faith. Furthermore, most of the educational and healing

institutions in the western world have originated in the
vision of Christian believers.

e. *On science.* Even science owes more to the Bible than is
generally supposed. The countries which have produced
the greatest advances in the industrial, medical and
technological fields are those in which Christianity has
been a dominant force. The fathers of modern science
were either Christians or respected Christian principles.
These include Johann Kepler (1571-1630), who dis-
covered the laws of planetary motion; Robert Boyle
(1627-1691), the father of modern chemistry; Sir Isaac
Newton (1642-1727), considered the greatest scientist that ever lived; Georges Cuvier (1769-1832), the
paleontologist; Louis Pasteur (1822-1895), the biologist
who gave the world the important processes of steriliza-
tion and pasteurization; and Wernher von Braun (1912-
1977), one of the world's top space scientists. Although
many modern scientists are atheists, little do they realize
that the inquisitive, creative atmosphere in which they
have worked has been produced by people whose religious roots are in the Bible.

f. *On people of all social classes.* The influence of the Bible
has not been limited to any one class of people. Men and
women from all walks of life have drawn inspiration from
it. Peasants and philosophers, doctors and factory
workers, salesmen and lawyers, scientists, musicians,
housewives and politicians from every conceivable back-
ground have turned to the Bible for the answers to life's
mysteries.

People of all ages, cultures and nations have welcomed
the Bible. It truly is a universal book. It has touched the
lives of men and women of every clime and colour, north,

south, east and west. The aged pore over its pages and treasure it. Young people turn to it for guidance. The Jesus movement of the 1960s and 1970s was a youth-led movement, and while the administration of most of the colleges and universities of modern America are humanistic, millions of young people are turning to Christ and are active in strong evangelical groups on campuses.

g. *On all the dimensions of the human personality.* Wherever the Bible has gone, it has uplifted man in every phase of his being: mentally, physically and spiritually. Those who follow the Bible learn to use their God-given powers of creativity and industry. Where the Bible is proclaimed the standard of living is inevitably raised and all sorts of ignorance are dispelled.

h. *It is the most studied book in the world.* More books have been written about the Bible than all other books put together. Many modern libraries contain tens of thousands of commentaries on the Bible alone. The Bible remains the best seller of all. In 1972 alone the United Bible Societies reported the sale of 218 million whole or parts of Bibles.

Two questions inevitably emerge to anyone who duly considers the facts:
   1. What claim does the Bible make for itself?
   2. What evidence is there that the claim is true?

The Bible is divided into two parts: the Old Testament and the New Testament. Writings of the Old Testament came through unique leaders known as 'prophets'. Writings of the New Testament were given through 'apostles', who were also prophets, and also other specially chosen writers.

The Bible claims to be an authoritative message from God

1. *This claim is found in the writings of the Old Testament prophets.* Acts 3:21 refers to the message 'which God has spoken by the mouth of all his holy prophets since the world began'. According to Deuteronomy 18:18 the true prophet receives his message from God. Verses 15-22 of that chapter should be studied carefully because they explain the basic nature of the prophetic office. Individually we see that the prophets who were the authors of Scripture claimed to be vehicles through which the Scriptures were conveyed, and they received their message from God. Here are a few examples.

    a. Moses (Num. 12:6-8)
    b. David (Mark 12:36; Acts 1:16)
    c. Isaiah (51:16; 59:21)
    d. Jeremiah (1:7-9)
    e. Ezekiel (3:4)
    f. Hosea (1:1)

2. *The same divine authority is claimed for the New Testament writers.*

    a. Luke (1 Tim. 5:18; Luke 10:7)
    b. John (1 John 4:6)
    c. Paul (1 Cor. 2:12-13)
    d. Peter (2 Peter 1:19-21)

3. *The inspiration of the Scriptures is defined.* It is a basic truth of the Christian faith and so it is important that it should be properly understood. The doctrine of the inspiration of the Scriptures simply teaches that the Holy Spirit of God so directed the human authors of the various books of the Bible that what they wrote was his infallible truth: a revelation of God's will to men. This does not mean that he

dictated his message to them like an executive dictating a letter to a secretary, for we can see the various personalities and styles of Scripture writers. God so worked not only to use their minds as instruments, but also utilizing their previous recollections and knowledge.

It is also important to note that God used different methods to convey information to those whom he chose to give his word. God spoke audibly to Moses (Num. 12:8). He communicated to Daniel through visions (Dan. 8:1), and inspired Paul through inner illuminations (1 Cor. 2:13). Regardless of the method God used to convey information to these instruments, *the result is the same*. What they wrote, that which makes up the 'canon' of Holy Scripture, is the Word of God. God guided, instructed and supervised them in such a manner that in the reception, retention and expression of God's message they were preserved from error.

Key Scripture passages on the meaning of inspiration

Throughout the Scriptures we find the writers claiming that they are proclaiming God's messages. Two passages are particularly critical in understanding what the Bible claims for itself.

1. *2 Timothy 3:16-17*. This is perhaps the fullest and most comprehensive statement on the truth of inspiration. It says, 'All Scripture is given by inspiration of God, and is profitable for doctrine, for reproof, for correction, for instruction in righteousness, that the man of God may be complete, thoroughly equipped for every good work.' Notice here that inspiration is *all-inclusive*. *All* Scripture is given by inspiration of God, not just a part of it. The word 'inspired' means 'God-breathed'. B. B. Warfield says, 'The "breath of God" is in Scripture just the symbol of His almighty power, the bearer of

His creative word.'[5] Here 'the breath of God' is used in a similar way to Psalm 33:6 where it describes God's act of creation.

2. *2 Peter 1:21.* Whereas 2 Timothy 3:16 states the basic fact of inspiration, 2 Peter 1:21 gives some indication of the relationship of the Holy Spirit to authors of Scripture. It says, 'For prophecy never came by the will of man, but holy men of God spoke as they were moved by the Holy Spirit.' This verse gives a *negative* and a *positive* statement relative to the origin of the Bible. Negatively, it did not come by the will of man. The word for 'came' (which is the same as 'moved' later in the verse) means to carry or bear. The assertion is that the Bible did not originate with the will of man — that is, with human wisdom, intellect or initiative. Although men were the vehicles through which truth came, it did not come from their minds originally. Positively, the text says, 'Holy men of God spoke as they were moved by the Holy Spirit.' In other words, the prophets and apostles were 'borne along' by the sovereign Spirit of God when they wrote the Bible. The Spirit guided, preserved, taught and supernaturally influenced their minds so that what they wrote was God's own mind for man.

Jesus Christ's use of the Old Testament Scriptures

Even a casual perusal of the Gospels shows that Christ accepted the statements of the Old Testament Scriptures as historically accurate and factually true. He obviously believed that the Hebrew Scriptures had supreme and unquestioned authority in matters of faith and morals.

1. Jesus *did not come to destroy the law and the prophets but to fulfil them.* 'Do not think that I came to destroy the Law or the Prophets. I did not come to destroy but to fulfil.

For assuredly, I say to you, till heaven and earth pass away, one jot or one tittle will by no means pass from the law till all is fulfilled' (Matt. 5:17-18). 'Jot' apparently refers to the little Hebrew letter 'yod', which looks like an apostrophe. It is the smallest letter in the Hebrew alphabet. 'Tittle' is believed by many scholars to refer to the little horn appearing on Hebrew letters. This shows how minutely detailed is God's inspiration and the great respect Christ had for the Scriptures.

2. Christ *appealed to Old Testament Scripture* as a source of doctrinal truth, historical fact and spiritual force (Matt. 7:12; 12:40; 13:14; 15:4; Mark 14:27; Luke 4:4, 8; 24:27). He accepted as fact such accounts as the creation of Adam and Eve (Matt. 19:4-5), the flood in the days of Noah (Matt. 24:37-39), the destruction of Sodom (Luke 17:28-29), and the swallowing of Jonah by the great fish (Matt. 12:40).

3. Jesus Christ distinctly *affirmed that God's Word is truth.* 'Sanctify them by your truth. Your word is truth' (John 17:17). This is a broad, comprehensive statement on the veracity of Scripture. Jesus believed that all that God had given through his prophets was truth — truth unmixed, truth unadulterated. Although the Bible contains a record of incorrect opinions of men, it is an inspired and accurate record of those opinions. For example, many of the opinions of Job's friends are a part of God's Word, but they are not necessarily the mind of God himself.

4. Jesus Christ *affirmed the infallibility of Scripture.* We have reserved for the last point the most conclusive, incontestable proof that Jesus accepted the Old Testament as God's inspired record. In John 10:35 we find Jesus saying, 'If he called them gods, to whom the word of God came (and the Scripture cannot be broken)...' etc. The statement

'the Scripture cannot be broken' is powerful. This means at least three things: the Scripture cannot be divided, disputed or destroyed. It cannot be divided because it is one unified whole. It cannot be disputed because every statement in it, whether it be doctrinal, geographical, scientific or historical, is true. It cannot be destroyed because God has pledged to preserve his Word for ever. Jesus said, 'Heaven and earth will pass away, but my words will by no means pass away' (Matt. 24:35).

The apostles mutually support each other

Not only did the various apostles claim to be inspired, but they bear witness to each other.

1. Peter affirmed Paul (2 Peter 3:15-16). He refers to the writings of Paul as 'Scripture'.

2. Paul affirms Luke (1 Tim. 5:18; Luke 10:7). Here Paul cites Luke's record of Jesus' statement 'The labourer is worthy of his wages' as Scripture.

3. Jude affirms Peter (Jude 17-18; 2 Peter 3:2-3). Jude refers to the words 'spoken before by the apostles of our Lord Jesus Christ'. This is a verbatim quote from Peter.

The conclusion we derive from the above evidence is that the Bible's claims to be the Word of God are historically and spiritually credible.

The truth of verbal inspiration

The question has been raised as to whether the very words of Scripture are inspired or merely the thoughts or concepts.

Verbal inspiration means inspiration of each single word of the Bible, as written in its original languages, Hebrew and Greek.

In favour of verbal inspiration, it should be noted that it is impossible to conceive of ideas apart from *words*. Any form of communication or even thought is framed in our minds as words. They are the building blocks that make up ideas. There can no more be ideas without words than there can be a sum without figures or a song without notes.

Paul claimed that the Holy Spirit gave him the very words to speak (1 Cor. 2:13). David said, 'The Spirit of the LORD spoke by me, and his word was on my tongue' (2 Sam. 23:2). Jeremiah affirmed, 'Then the LORD put forth his hand and touched my mouth, and the LORD said to me: "Behold, I have put my words in your mouth"' (1:9).

Proofs of the Bible's claim

The fourth question of the *Westminster Larger Catechism* asks: 'How does it appear the Scriptures are the word of God?' The answer given states: 'The Scriptures manifest themselves to be the word of God, by their majesty and purity; by the consent of all the parts, and the scope of the whole, which is to give all glory to God; by their light and power to convince and convert sinners, to comfort and build up believers unto salvation. But the Spirit of God, bearing witness by and with the Scriptures in the heart of man, is alone able fully to persuade it that they are the very word of God.'

J. I. Packer points out in a commentary on this statement that Scripture is always the best evidence for itself, and that more good is done by simply preaching biblical truth in the power of the Holy Spirit than arguing to bring faith in the Bible's inspiration. With this I agree. However, we can assume that every truth of God is in harmony with human reason (though it certainly transcends human reason) and is historically factual. Although the Word of God bears the aspect of credibility and truthfulness on the very face of it, we believe that the following evidences of the trustworthiness of Scripture are important.

The unity of Scripture

The Bible was written in three languages on two continents and its compilation extended through the slow process of sixteen centuries. It was written at different times and under the most varying of circumstances. It had forty different authors from diverse backgrounds. Among those God chose to write his word were farmers, fishermen, kings, soldiers, shepherds, scribes and a doctor. It was written in such diverse places as tents, deserts, cities, palaces and dungeons. Yet, wonder of wonders, in spite of this diversity, it is *one book*. It contains one message, one code of ethics, one system of doctrine and one plan of salvation.

A. W. Pink gives the following interesting comparison to illustrate the marvel of the unity of Scripture. 'Imagine forty persons of different nationalities, possessing various degrees of musical culture visiting the organ of some cathedral and at long intervals of time, and without any collusion whatever, striking sixty-six different notes, which when combined yielded the theme of the grandest oratorio ever heard: would it not show that behind these forty different men there was one presiding mind, one great Tonemaster?'[6]

It is not claimed, of course, that there are no difficulties or seeming contradictions in the Scriptures. Nor would we argue for the *simplicity* of every truth taught in the Bible. What we *do* claim is that there are no real contradictions in the Bible and when it is properly interpreted in the true context, it is internally harmonious and consistent.

The character of the teachings of the Bible

The Bible is not the only book that seeks to set forth a system of religion, but it is incomparably more noble, elevated and spiritually divine than any other.

1. *Its concept of God.* The ancient gods who were extolled by heathen writers are represented as fickle, vengeful, lustful; in short, carnal like their creators. The gods of the oriental religions are impersonal, mystical and utterly unworthy of worship. But, in contrast, the God of Scripture is glorious in holiness, power, grace and sovereignty, in every way worthy of the adoration of his creatures. The biblical description of God wears on its very face the aspect of verity, for men left to themselves do not create such concepts.

2. *Its concept of man.* The Bible gives an honest, realistic picture of mankind. It describes man as being created in the image of God, the most glorious of all creatures on earth, reflecting the Almighty in his intelligence, dominance of the world and creativity. But unlike other religions, which flatter man and exalt his 'moral dignity', the Bible pictures human nature as fallen, corrupt and polluted by sin. Even the principal characters of the Bible, whose virtues are models in many areas of life, are not excepted.

3. *Its concept of salvation.* We find in the Bible God's marvellous plan to rescue man out of his sin and misery. It reveals how God, out of his sovereign goodness, had mercy upon mankind and devised a plan of salvation for them. This plan involved the coming of God himself to earth in the person of his Son Jesus Christ, who lived a perfect life to set an example for men and finally died for their sins upon the cross. He rose again from the dead, ascended into the presence of God and lives to bestow his gifts upon thos'

who seek him. The Bible tells of how through faith in Christ
the greatest sinners can be completely forgiven of all their
sins and have the righteousness of Christ imputed to
them. The Bible also prophesies that Jesus will come again
and receive his people unto eternal glory, giving some insight into the nature of that glorious abode which he has
prepared for them. This remarkable revelation is totally
unlike and infinitely above all the schemes of religion devised by man.

4. *Its concept of ethics.* In the Bible we find a gradually
unfolding code of conduct that is designed for the maximum
happiness and well-being of human beings who live on
earth. It roots in the ethics of the Hebrew people who were
given the Ten Commandments, a comprehensive system
of morals that governs every aspect of life. In the New Testament this code is completed and broadened by the teachings of Jesus Christ and his apostles. It teaches individual
people how to attain a proper self-awareness and live in
harmony with their Creator. It provides an ethical code of
living for people in all walks of life. It exalts legitimate
human government and shows its importance in maintain-
ing order among men. It establishes monogamy, the highest and best condition for people in marital relations, and
instructs all the members of the family as to what their
proper conduct should be in all their mutual relations.

It is true that those who profess the name of Christ have
not always been consistent in their adherence to his
teachings. But this is the fault of the adherents to the code
not the code itself. Some have claimed that Christianity has
failed to provide the stability and peace that the world needs.
But the truth is that Christianity has not failed, it simply
has not been tried, in the fullest sense. To the extent that it
has been practised, the 'good society' envisioned by man
has come about. Christianity not only condemns the

oppression of the poor, war and crime, but also provides a power to resist these temptations. Unfortunately, the basically evil tendencies of human nature have usually overwhelmed the high goals of the Christian faith.

Fulfilled prophecy

The Bible teems with prophecies about nations, individuals and the world as a whole. Some of these have been fulfilled and some are now being fulfilled. This remarkable fact should show to any unprejudiced person that the author of the Bible is not of this earth. Here are some examples.

1. *Nations of the world.* In Daniel 2:31-35 there is a prophecy which embraces events that came about many hundreds of years after the prophet Daniel who lived in the sixth century before Christ. In this passage, using the special gift God gave him, Daniel is interpreting a dream of the Babylonian King Nebuchadnezzar. The king's dream consisted of a vision of a great image, which had a head of gold, chest and arms of silver, thighs of brass, legs of iron and feet mixed with iron and clay. The vision pictures four great kingdoms, which were to rise in succession, only the first existing in dominance at the time Daniel was living. The head of gold was Babylon (606-536 B. C.). The breast and arms of silver represented Medo-Persia (536-330 B. C.). The belly and thighs of bronze refer to the Grecian empire (330-43 B. C.). The legs of iron and feet of iron and clay symbolized the Roman Empire (43 B. C.). The two legs and set of feet represented the divided state of the Roman Empire, which did in fact separate into two separate units, with Rome and Constantinople as their capitals. This division was recognized by the emperor Valentinian in A. D. 364.

The four great civil and military powers are also portrayed in chapter 7 of Daniel under the figure of four beasts: a lion, a bear, a leopard and another beast of terrible appearance. The last beast had ten horns, symbolizing the fragmentation of the Roman Empire. Among these ten horns another horn, a 'little one', arose. The break up of the great Roman Empire has taken place exactly as Daniel prophesied, and the modern state of Europe with its many nations is the result of this dissolution. The little horn refers to the Antichrist.

2. *Prophecies concerning Israel.* Many amazing prophecies concerning the nation Israel are found in the Scriptures. The dispersion of Israel throughout the world as a result of her disobedience to God is predicted in Deuteronomy 28:64. This took place in a preliminary way during the Babylonian captivity, but happened in a much fuller sense after the destruction of Jerusalem in A. D. 70. Hosea gives a remarkable description of the condition of the Jewish people between the time they lost their capital and their national recovery in 1948. 'My God will cast them away, because they did not obey him; and they shall be wanderers among the nations' (9:17). No better expression could possibly describe the Jewish people during these many centuries than 'wanderers among the nations'.

The return of Israel to its homeland was also prophesied in many places in the Bible (see Isa. 11:11-12; Ezek. 28:25; 36:24; 38:8; 39:27-28; Zech. 2:12; 8:7-8; 10:9-10).

3. *The destruction of Israel's chief city*, Jerusalem, is predicted in Daniel 9:26. This prophecy was made during the Babylonian captivity when the city was in ruins.

4. *Prophecies concerning Jesus Christ*

a. His coming into the world. In Genesis 3:15 Christ is set forth as the 'seed of the woman' who would crush the head of Satan. In Genesis 49:10 it is said that the Saviour would descend from the tribe of Judah. Psalm 132:11 says that he would be a descendant of David.

b. The time of his coming. In Daniel 9:25-26 it is stated that 483 years would elapse between 'the going forth of the command to restore and build Jerusalem' until the coming of the Messiah. This segment of time is divided into two sections of 7 years and 62 years. This probably allows for some lapse of time after seven years when the prophetic clock stops. The first command to rebuild Jerusalem took place under Cyrus in 538 B. C. This injunction was for a time suspended, but in 445 B. C. Artaxerxes I commissioned Nehemiah to complete the reconstruction of the city. Many scholars see this as the date referred to by Daniel (see p. 168).

c. The place where he was to be born, Bethlehem (Micah 5:2).

d. His miraculous virgin birth (Isa. 7:14).

e. His humble origins (Isa. 53:2-3).

f. His substitutionary death (Isa. 53:8; Dan. 9:26).

g. His experiences on the cross (Ps. 22:7; 69:21).

h. His burial in a rich man's grave (Isa. 53:9).

i. His resurrection (Ps. 16:10-11).

j. The worldwide acceptance of his message. In Genesis 22:18 it is prophesied that in the seed of Abraham all nations would be blessed. Isaiah 11:10 and 42:6 state that the Gentiles would believe in the Messiah. This is fulfilled in the spread of the Christian faith through all nations. The universal dominion of Jesus is enlarged upon in Psalm 72.

The inside argument for the Bible's inspiration

This has significance, of course, only to Christians, who know that the Bible is the Word of God because of the witness of the Spirit. This experience is related to the anointing or

'unction from the Holy One', as taught in 1 John 2:20, 27:
'But you have an anointing from the Holy One, and you
know all things'; 'But the anointing which you have received
from him abides in you, and you do not need that anyone
teach you; but as the same anointing teaches you concerning
all things, and is true...' etc. There is a dynamic rapport between the Christian and his Bible that is impossible for one
not related to God to understand. He knows God speaks to
him through its teachings. He sees its promises fulfilled in
his life over and over. To him the Bible is a living book.
When he opens and reads it God providentially leads him to
passages that suit his daily needs. This is the most meaningful
'proof' of Scripture of all. It is actually all the believer needs.

The Bible and the human dilemma

John Wesley sets forth the options a human being faces as
he considers the authority of the Bible.

> I beg leave to propose a short, clear, and strong argu-
> ment to prove the divine inspiration of the Holy
> Scriptures. The Bible must be the invention either of
> good men or angels, bad men or devils, or of God.
> 1. It could not be the invention of good men or angels;
>   for they neither would nor could make a book, and
>   tell lies all the time they were writing it, saying,
>   "Thus saith the Lord," when it was their own
>   invention.
> 2. It could not be the invention of bad men or devils;
>   for they would not make a book which commands
>   all duty, forbids all sin, and condemns their souls
>   to hell to all eternity.
> 3. Therefore, I draw this conclusion, that the Bible
>   must be given by divine inspiration.[7]

3.
Learning about man

As we have already seen, the Bible tells us that man is a creature of God. It clearly teaches that he is unique among all
God's creation here on earth. David the psalmist said, 'I will
praise you, for I am fearfully and wonderfully made' (Ps.
139:14). Unquestionably, mankind is the crowning jewel of
God's handiwork on earth. The fact that God has shown so
much attention to him in his moral government and plan of
salvation leads us to think that God has favoured man even
above the angels. Man is made 'a little lower than the angels'
in that his habitat is earth not heaven, but still he is 'crowned
... with glory and honour' (Ps. 8:5).

The dignity and uniqueness of man is expressed forcibly
in the comprehensive statement that he is made in the image
of God (Gen. 1:27; 1 Cor. 11:7; James 3:9). An image is a likeness. As the still water of a lake reflects the likeness of one
who looks into it, so a human being exhibits something of
the glory of his Creator.

The likeness of man to God in the original creation

A study of this question shows that there are two aspects of
the image of God in man, one of which has been defaced by

the Fall, one of which has not. There is a *natural* likeness to God that refers to his rational faculties: personality, self-consciousness and self-determination. This is all rooted in the fact that a human being has an invisible, spiritual and immortal part of his being known as the soul. Animals of the brute creation have life but not personality.

There was also a *moral* likeness to God, which the original man and woman had, and that is holiness or freedom from sin. These two aspects of mankind in the original creation need to be considered separately.

Natural likeness to God

1. *Man has a rational soul.* That the human person is physical is obvious. The body is visible and tangible. According to the Bible he also has a soul which can exist in a conscious state apart from the body, although there is a certain incompleteness in the soul or spirit in that state. Jesus said that the soul is 'spiritual', having neither flesh nor bones (Luke 24:39).

a. The reality of the soul is often cited in Scripture. Genesis 2:7 is the account of the original donation of life to man. When God breathed into man he became a living being. As a living being he not only has a body (which can be killed), but also a soul, which only God can destroy, meaning 'ruin' (Matt. 10:28). The apostle John prayed for the 'soul' prosperity of believers, along with good health (3 John 2).

b. The soul can exist in a conscious state apart from the body. In Scripture death is the departure of soul from body (Gen. 35:18; James 2:26); and life returns when the soul comes back (1 Kings 17:22; Luke 8:55). The body can be killed but the soul cannot (Matt. 10:28). The body is described as a tent (2 Peter 1:14), a house (2 Cor. 5:1), or a temple (John 2:21) in which a human being lives. Like a garment it can be cast off (2 Cor. 5:4).

Paul had an experience which he said could have been 'out of the body' (2 Cor. 12:2). Lazarus and Dives died and experienced pleasure and pain respectively in heaven and hell (Luke 16:19-31). The dying thief was promised a place with Christ after death in paradise (Luke 23:43). Paul expressed a desire to depart and be with Christ after death, which would not have been possible if the soul could not exist apart from the body (Phil. 1:21-23). There are also other references to the fact that a disembodied state after death is possible. In the spiritual scene around Mount Zion described by the writer of Hebrews, 'the spirits of just men made perfect' are mentioned (Heb. 12:23). John saw in his vision of the fifth seal 'the souls of those who had been slain for the word of God' (Rev. 6:9).

2. *The soul is immortal.* Since God is the creator of the soul, presumably God could destroy or annihilate it if he pleased, but that he does not do so is evident from the fact that everlasting life and happiness is promised to the righteous (Matt. 25:46; John 5:24), and death and misery to the wicked (Matt. 25:46; Rev. 14:11). Matthew 10:28 refers to the destruction of soul and body in hell. However, destruction is not annihilation or cessation of existence. If everlasting life means everlasting happiness, everlasting death means everlasting misery.

3. *Are the spirit and the soul separate entities?* Passages such as 1 Thessalonians 5:23 and Hebrews 4:12 seem to imply that there is in fact a difference. But what is this difference? There seems to be no valid distinction as far as their essence is concerned. Genesis 41:8 says Pharaoh's spirit was troubled.

Psalm 42:6 states that David's soul was 'cast down'. These passages seem to convey the same meaning. Soul and spirit appear to be interchangeable when referring to the trauma in the heart of Jesus (John 12:27; 13:21). The difference in soul and spirit is evidently functional rather than essential.

4. *Faculties of the soul.* Man's responsibility to the Creator is based on his intellectual and moral nature, or perhaps we could say his psychology. We believe that there is a three-fold division in the human personality.

a. *Intellect, the power to think.* The cognitive faculty implies self-awareness and the ability to reason abstractly. By his creation man can think about himself, the world around him and God. Through the brain the spirit is able to store information, thus memory.

b. *The affections or sensitivity, the power to feel.* Man is an emotional as well as a rational or intellectual being. Through what we refer to as the affections, man has the power to love, hate, fear, relish, rejoice, grieve, etc.

c. *The will, the power to choose.* Man's power to choose is the most glorious and yet at the same time the most awesome of his capacities. Upon his free choices rides his own destiny as well as the happiness and misery of others who are under his influence.

How are the mind, the affections and the will related? Which takes priority? What we choose brings information into the intellect. But choice is obviously influenced by the sensitivities or affections. These are in turn influenced by the mind. In other words, the will chooses that which the affections prefer, and the affections are developed through the stimulation that comes through the mind. We conclude that the mind has been designed by the Creator to have the uppermost position in the spirit. But these three faculties are interrelated. It is important to know that the will cannot be separated from the mind and the affections. The sense in which it is free will be considered later.

d. *The conscience*. Strictly speaking, the conscience should not be considered a separate faculty any more than the memory or the intuition. It seems that conscience involves the combined action of all three faculties, especially intellect and sensibility. Conscience has been defined as 'self-consciousness in relation to moral government'. It is the self-judgement of the soul in relation to moral behaviour and responsibility. The importance of the conscience is seen in the fact that it is an important element in man's moral government. The purpose of the conscience is to bear witness. To the extent that it reflects correct views in the mind, which depends upon proper instruction, it places man under responsibility and will be a source of either 'excusing' or 'accusing' (Rom. 2:15). The book of conscience may be one of the books opened by God at the final judgement (Rev. 20:12).

Man's dominion over the earth

It is interesting to note that the first place in the Bible where man is said to be made in the image of God (Gen. 1:26) this affirmation is made in connection with his dominion over all other forms of life on earth. God's original commission to Adam, the first man, was to 'be fruitful and multiply; fill the earth and subdue it' (Gen. 1:28). This commission to the patriarch of the human family has never been withdrawn. The command to subdue the earth is comprehensive. It means to explore the depths of knowledge in the universe, to search for truth, and to harness the resources of earth for the human family. It would appear that man has been incredibly tardy in carrying out this mandate. The fields of human knowledge, scientific research and exploration have been hindered by stupidity, superstition and prejudice. The Bible teaches that this is because of sin. Nonetheless, the work goes on. Without question the God-given genius of the human intellect has flowered in the past 300 years especially. Modern scientific, technological and medical advance is an exercise of his dominion over this world (see Ps. 8).

From a Christian perspective the marvellous intellectual capacities of man have been perverted and diverted too frequently for abuse and moral evil. Nonetheless, we must admire the achievements of men who have been placed under God's creation mandate. All the abilities of men, such as artistic, musical, military and political achievements, demonstrate his likeness to God who is the supreme creative genius.

Man's spiritual likeness to God in creation, holiness

1. *Man (Adam) was placed under God's moral law*. From Matthew 19:19 and Romans 13:9 we learn that man's duty has two aspects: his relation to God, and his relation to his fellow men. This duty can be summed up in love: love to the Creator, *Yahweh*; and love to his intelligent creature: man. Love to God means supreme regard to him in his infinite perfection: adoration of his person, obedience to his commands, and submission to his will. To love God means to seek to promote God's glory as the only one who is supremely worthy of praise.

Since man's responsibility is twofold, Godward and manward, after Eve was created for Adam the second dimension in his life was complete. Now he could fulfil his duties both to the Creator and to a fellow creature, his wife. The multiplication of the human race through Adam and Eve proportionately increased their responsibility to humanity, in this case their own offspring.

After his creation, man became the object of God's attention and favour. God heaped blessings on Adam in every way and thus manifested his love. But the relationship of God and Adam was such that a moral government was established, with God assuming the role of father, friend and judge. Man was a child, companion and subject. As the Creator, God was sovereign over Adam and demanded from him supreme allegiance.

Genesis 2 describes Adam's position in the world God gave him. A part of his responsibility was abstinence from the 'tree of the knowledge of good and evil' (v. 9). This injunction was a test of Adam's loyalty and obedience. The accompanying warning 'in the day that you eat of it you shall surely die' (v. 17) was a natural and inevitable outgrowth of moral government. Responsible creatures can expect reward for obedience and punishment for disobedience. The angels are also under moral government, as seen by the fact that the disobedient angels were expelled from heaven.

2. *Man's responsibility is based on his natural likeness to God.* We call this free agency. Man's endowment of intellect, sensibility and will, combined with conscience, the monitor of his moral behaviour, placed him in a unique and exalted position upon earth. But this high honour placed him also in a position of having momentous responsibilities. The power to know, love and choose God also carried with it the potential to reject and despise him. This moral dignity and freedom is man's glory and potential shame.

It is evident that God made man fully capable of doing his will. He had every faculty, that is, the mental and moral equipment necessary to render supreme devotion to his glorious Creator and Benefactor. The demands upon Adam were reasonable and suitable to his endowments. Nothing was required of him beyond his power to fulfil. Amidst all the blessings and benefits, there was only one prohibition. In the utopian environment of the Garden of Eden it would seem that loyalty to God would have been natural and easy for Adam and Eve.

3. *Adam was created holy.* Not only was the first man con-stitutionally equipped to do God's will, he also possessed a righteous nature. Over and over again, the result of God's creative handiwork is pronounced 'good'. If this was true physically of the material creation, how much more so of Adam, the one made in God's image. His mind, heart and will were in a perfectly ordered condition. His intellect was enlightened by an understanding of God and his works. His heart was set upon God and his wife. His will was exercised in choosing the things God approved. No cloud of iniquity marred his communion with his Maker. This point is brought out in Ecclesiastes 7:29: 'Truly, this only I have found: that God made man upright, but they have sought out many schemes.' The man who came forth from God needed no 'recall' from the manufacturer. He was perfect. But as the text in Ecclesiastes says, men have sought out many schemes and perverted the creation of God.

Notwithstanding all his endowments man was in a state of trial and fallibility. God had assured him of no permanent happiness except by perfect obedience. This fallibility proved to be the cause of Adam's subsequent lapse, a calamity that befell him and all his descendants.

The fall of man

The human race is derived from Adam and Eve, and thus all the common physical, spiritual and constitutional character-istics of the human race are derived from Adam through the natural birth. Like gives rise to like. That moral as well as physical characteristics are transmitted is evident from Scrip-ture and experience. This fact opens up a vast area of study and touches on the foundations of God's dealings with man. The pollution of the human family through connection with Adam is called original sin.

Adam was the representative man

The Bible recognizes the fact of personal identity. There is a certain sense in which people are dealt with strictly as individuals. But in another sense the Bible refers to *race* responsibility and *race* guilt. In other words, the Bible teaches racial unity.

The name Adam comes from the Hebrew spelling of that word, referring to the first man. The word is also used throughout the Old Testament for man generically (Ps. 144:3; Prov. 29:23). It is interesting to note that *Adam* refers not to men in kind but to a collective group of men (see Jonah 4:11, where the word is translated *persons*). The word Adam has no plural, pointing to the unity of the race. For example, in Proverbs 28:28, which says, 'When the wicked arise, men hide themselves', the word for men is in the Hebrew *adam*—singular.

The unity of the human family is taught also in Acts 17:26: 'And he has made from one blood every nation of men to dwell on all the face of the earth, and has determined their preappointed times and the boundaries of their dwellings.'

Adam's sinful nature was communicated to his progeny

A universal effect or result points to a universal cause. The human race is in uniform revolt against God. We do not find people coming into the world going in different directions spiritually, but all are bent towards sin, sometimes in spite of the best environment and education. According to Romans 3:23 all have sinned and come short of the glory of God. This universal sin of man is voluntary, deliberate and conscious, but the fact that it is universal points to a common source.

This common source, according to the Bible, is the sinful nature derived from Adam. That man is born with a polluted nature is clear from such passages as Psalm 51:5; Psalm 58:3; and Ephesians 2:3. These verses lead us to conclude that corruption is latent even in infants and waits only consciousness and mental development for more mature exercise. Sin arises from the human personality certainly but not necessarily, in other words it is by choice. Man's free agency is not changed by the Fall, it is just that his agency is directed against God's will. Does this mean that 'free will' is implied in human nature? If by free will is meant that man chooses voluntarily and not from compulsion, it is true. If free will means that human nature is neutral towards morality, and is as likely to choose good as evil, then it is false. The will is a part of the human personality. It cannot be separated from the ruling dispositions of man's nature.

Human experience backs up what the Bible teaches on original sin. The conduct of infants and children proves this. They do not need to be taught to sin. Selfishness, pride and rebellion against authority are instinctive to them. This fact is also demonstrated in the experience of Christians. The way sin arises in the believer shows that it is deep inner psychology, not just by overt act. Believers are conscious of jealousy, enmity, lust etc., which arise spontaneously when they are confronted with temptations. This sinful tendency derived from Adam is called the flesh (Gal. 5:16-21). Paul referred to the indwelling of sin in Romans 7:23 and called it a 'law ... in my members' bringing him into bondage. If the most godly of people are conscious of this problem, then it surely is a *principle,* rooted in their very being.

All men sinned in Adam

While Scripture teaches the unity of all men, it also recognizes the uniqueness of Adam as the public head of the human race, acting, as it were, on behalf of all. The representative principle is taught in the Bible. Future generations bear the consequences of the sin of their ancestors (see Exod. 20:5). Achan's family shared in the judgement caused by his thieving (Josh. 7:24). No doubt they were sympathetic with him. Hebrews 7:9-10 states that Levi paid tithes 'in the loins of his father Abraham', in other words, what Abraham did, in a sense Levi did. The supreme application of this principle is seen in the relationship of the two men Adam and Christ, with the people joined to them. The sin of one and the righteousness of the other bring men into condemnation and justification respectively.

Sometimes it is said that Adam's sin was imputed to the human race. This is true if properly understood. It is not that men are blamed for what Adam did (any more than believers can be praised for what Christ did). It is just that because of their organic union with him and common nature with him, men are counted and treated as having done what Adam did. Indeed, they have done so in reality. At the dawn of consciousness all Adam's family voluntarily sin against God's law.

The most complete statement in Scripture on the relationship of Adam's sin to men is Romans 5:12-21. Verse 12 is the key. It says, 'Therefore, just as through one man sin entered the world, and death through sin, and thus death spread to all men, because all sinned.' 'Because' ('for that' in the Authorized Version) could be translated 'in whom'. This corresponds to 1 Corinthians 15:22: 'in Adam all die'.

Clearly from these truths of Scripture we can see that through Adam humanity is fallen and spiritually desolated. But the infinite wisdom of the Creator is still visible. The ruins of ancient civilizations, such as those of Egypt, Greece and Rome, can still be seen and of course attract tourists from all over the world. In many cases, such as the castles built by the crusaders, or the Roman Forum and Coliseum, the ravages of time have taken their toll. The roofs are gone, the walls and pillars are partially collapsed, and even the stones are decayed by the rains and winds of many centuries. And yet, in spite of this deterioration, the glory of the ancient civilizations, especially the genius of those who designed and built these buildings, is still in evidence.

So it is with mankind. The men and women of Adam's race are obviously fallen. From a spiritual standpoint, human nature is in ruins. But the glory and wisdom of the Creator is seen in the very constitution of man.

What mankind did not lose by the Fall

1. *He did not lose the faculties of his soul.* From a merely physical or 'mechanical' standpoint, nothing has changed. Even fallen man has a mind to reason, emotions with which to love or hate, and a will to choose.

2. *Free moral agency.* All rational beings are moral agents: God, angels and men. All are free in the sense that they act without compulsion, with voluntary free choice.

3. *Conscience.* John 1:9 says that Jesus is the light which lights every man coming into the world. This seems to refer

to the natural knowledge of the Creator, and the conscience that results from it.

4. *Responsibility*. Because man is still a moral agent, under law, he is accountable to the Creator.

5. *The salutary effects of God's common grace*. Human beings can have a natural 'goodness', that is, positive qualities before their fellow man. This comes about through the restraints of society, fear of punishment, prickings of conscience and natural affection.

What mankind did lose by the Fall

1. *He lost his original righteousness before God*. Spiritually speaking, all aspects of man's nature, that is, all his faculties, have been affected by his participation in Adam's fall.

a. *The mind has been corrupted*. In Ephesians 4:18 the apostle states that the mind of the natural man is darkened, and this darkness of mind is through 'ignorance' and 'blindness' of heart. As we can easily see, the human intellect can soar to great heights in all realms of investigation in the natural world. The laws of mathematics, physics, chemistry, language, and certainly the facts of history can be understood, depending upon the capacities of the individual mind. Even historical facts of the Bible can be comprehended without special illumination. But this power does not extend to spiritual discernment (Rom. 3:11; 1 Cor. 2:14-15).

b. *The affections have been disordered and perverted*. The natural facility of human nature to love or hate, to delight in or despise, is sometimes referred to as the emotions. Fallen man does not naturally love God, but rather despises and hates him. Romans 8:7 says that the carnal mind is enmity against God and is not subject to his law. Its motives are selfish, earthly and sensual (see Eph. 2:3). This was recognized in the times of Job who said that man is abominable, filthy and 'drinks iniquity like water' (15:16). This tendency can, of course, gradually grow worse to the point that human affections are 'vile' and perverted (Rom. 1:26).

c. *The capacity of choosing is misdirected.* Natural men can and often do choose to do things that are good in themselves, such as paying debts, going to church, etc. But they will never choose God as the ultimate goal of life, or love him supremely. All actions, even those not inherently evil, are rooted in selfishness. Lost souls will not even come to the remedy of salvation, which is Jesus Christ (John 5:40; Acts 13:46). To the self-righteous, Christ is a stumbling block, to the worldly-wise and intellectual, he is foolishness (1 Cor. 1:23).

d. *The outward conduct of men is according to their nature.* Romans 3 gives an extended description of how fallen man uses the bodily members (eyes, hands, feet, etc.) to perpetuate iniquity.

e. Since all true righteousness must be rooted in love to God, and the natural man is devoid of this quality, we can say and say truly that *he is totally depraved.* That is, in so far as true obedience to God is concerned, he has not one shred of righteousness to recommend himself to God. Even his pushing of a plough is 'sin' in view of the fact that everything man does should spring from desire to glorify God (Prov. 21:4).

2. *He lost the favour of God.* As the Creator, God of course loves men, fallen or unfallen, viewed as the offspring of his hands. But as the judge of the universe God is against sin and sinners. He has pronounced that through sin all are condemned. In Romans 5 we find the word *condemnation* several times in reference to man's state. This is a legal term indicating that man is a criminal who has been convicted in the court of heaven with the threat of eternal separation from God hanging over his head. God's displeasure against those who have broken his law is called his *wrath* (John 3:36; Romans 1:18). The place known as hell, eternal separation from God, was made for the devil and his angels, but man heads in that direction through rebellion against his Creator.

3. *He lost the fellowship of God.* Fellowship with God was broken in the Garden of Eden. Adam was expelled from the presence of God and the flaming sword blazing above the garden symbolized the broken fellowship. Paul describes the state of the Ephesians prior to conversion as 'aliens from the commonwealth of Israel and strangers from the covenants of promise, having no hope and without God in the world' (2:12). Sinners are enemies of God (Rom. 5:10) and in need of reconciliation (2 Cor. 5:19).

4. *He lost his ability to deliver himself.* There are different types of ability and inability. There is physical ability. 'His ankle is broken and he cannot play in the game tonight.' There is also a kind of mental or moral inability, as when Joseph's brothers *could not* speak peaceably to him (Gen. 37:4). 'I cannot eat this salad without dressing.' Inability is often used in Scripture to note a voluntary aversion or permanent choice or disinclination. This can even be attributed to God. God cannot lie (Titus 1:2) or deny himself (2 Tim. 2:13). Christ

'could not' do works in Nazareth because of the unbelief of
the people (Mark 6:5). Christians 'cannot' sin because they
have the seed of God in them (1 John 3:9). Evil men 'cannot'
do good, or come to God (Josh. 24:19; John 6:44; Rom. 8:8;
Heb. 3:19).

Certainly God will not require anybody to do anything that
is naturally or physically impossible. Nor will God require
anybody to do that which they have no opportunity or means
to do. But he can and does hold people responsible for doing
what by creation they were capable of doing, but because of a
nature hostile to him they are now unwilling to do.

Summary

The Bible teaches and experience confirms that God created
man in a holy and upright state but through voluntary rebellion (originally in the head Adam and personally through
choice) he has become a depraved creature, alienated and
hostile to God. Although he still retains some of the original
endowments given him, and still reflects in some respects
the glory of his Maker, man is affected in all the parts of his
being by sin. His intellect is darkened, his affections are
corrupted, and his will is inclined to evil. He is condemned,
lost and hopeless apart from some initiative of God to recover
him.

4.
Learning about the gospel

In order for man to be recovered or saved from his fallen state two great problems have to be solved. One is an objective, legal problem, having to do with his state before God. The other is personal and subjective, having to do with his actual condition (nature, attitudes, etc.). Since the Fall, man's legal state is one of condemnation. He is a sinner, convicted in the court of heaven and condemned to eternal separation from God. In order to be restored to the favour and fellowship of the Creator, this guilt, the source of estrangement, must be removed.

The personal or practical difficulty has to do with man's sinful corrupt nature. He is a rebel against heaven, hostile to his Creator, bent on pursuing selfish and base ends. The whole human race are sinners by nature, choice and habit. God cannot enter into communion with anyone in this condition.

Viewed from a human standpoint, that is, looking at the problem purely from natural reason, the situation seems hopeless. There is nothing that man can do to recover himself from the pit into which he has fallen. But the Bible reveals a glorious plan of God, who steps into the picture to solve the problem of sin and to rescue man from his impending destruction.

The Old Testament doctrine of redemption

The mercy of God was demonstrated in the Garden of Eden

The first intimation that God would move in grace and mercy towards men is found in the Garden of Eden. The dark cloud of guilt and judgement hung over the first pair, Adam and Eve. But God *came* to Adam, *calling him* by his name and *entering into dialogue* with him about his sin. Although Adam and Even received appropriate chastisement for their sin, embodied in the curse against the serpent was a promise of deliverance against the serpent's influence (Gen. 3:15). Soon God provided a way for Adam to be clothed after he became conscious of his nakedness. Thus the first blood shed on earth was in connection with a remedy and covering for fallen man.

The way of salvation was set forth in the Old Testament sacrifices

Starting with the offering of Abel the Old Testament worship consistently featured the offering and sacrifice of animals. Noah offered burnt offerings (Gen. 8:20-21). Job was instructed to offer sacrifices for his friends (42:8). Abraham's family religion included altar sacrifices, such as the offering of a ram on Mount Moriah, in the place of his son (Gen. 22:12). The deliverance of the children of Israel from Egypt was accompanied by the slaying of a male lamb of the first year, whose blood was to be sprinkled on the posts of the houses (Exod. 12:7).

Elaborate rituals of sacrifice were included in the Mosaic law. There were offerings made in the outer court of the tabernacle by individual worshippers (Lev. 1:4-5). On the great Day of Atonement two goats were involved in sacrifice, offerings which were made by the high priest acting in an official capacity. By the casting of the lots one was to be a 'scapegoat', the other was designated a 'sin offering' (Lev. 16:9-10). Upon the head of the scapegoat the priest laid his hands and confessed the sins of the people. Then the victim was sent alone into the arid desert to waste away (Lev. 16:21-22). The sin offering goat was to be killed and brought within the veil, its blood being sprinkled upon the mercy seat (v. 15). This offering was an 'atonement' for the 'uncleanness', 'transgressions' and 'sins' of the people (v. 16). The word atonement (*caphar*) originally meant 'cover' (akin to the word 'pitch' in Gen. 6:14). It came to be used in the sense of 'hide' in reference to man's sin, or 'purge away' (Ps. 65:3, AV) and 'forgive' (Jer. 18:23, AV). *Caphar* carried with it the idea of appeasement, that is, the turning away of God's displeasure (Ezek. 16:63), and also reconciliation (Dan. 9:24).

The two prominent ideas in the Old Testament sacrifices were *satisfaction,* that is, making full reparation to offended deity; and *substitution,* the transfer of guilt to an innocent victim.

The New Testament gives a complete revelation about the person and teachings of Jesus Christ

The New Testament teaches that the Old Testament promises of a Saviour are fulfilled in the person of Jesus Christ who gave himself as a sacrifice for sin. This is indicated in the message of John the Baptist who introduced Christ. His exclamation, 'Behold! The Lamb of God who takes away the sin of the world!' (John 1:29), points to the fact that Christ was the antitype of the Passover lamb. He is referred to in Hebrews as the priest who would offer himself as a sacrifice for sin (Heb. 4:14; 7:26-27). Jesus claimed to be the 'anointed one' signifying the Messiah, the promised deliverer of Israel

(Luke 4:18; John 4:25-26). The priestly work of Christ is only one aspect of his ministry. It will be helpful for us to examine in broad outline what the New Testament teaches about the person and work of Christ.

The New Testament teachings about the person of Christ

Jesus was and is God

This point has already been proved (see p. 23).

Jesus was and is a real man

Early in church history there was a heresy known as docetism, which taught that Jesus did not have a real human body. It grew out of the Gnostic view that evil is inherent in the physical body. But Jesus had a real body which experienced all the limitations and trials of men, apart from sin (Heb. 4:15). Jesus also had a human soul or spirit (Matt. 26:38; John 11:33; John 19:30). He shared in normal physical experiences, such as growth (Luke 2:52), hunger (Matt. 4:2), and weariness (John 4:6). He also demonstrated ordinary human emotional qualities, such as love (Mark 10:21), compassion (Matt. 9:36), anger (Mark 3:5), sadness (John 11:33), and dread (John 12:27).

Not only was Jesus' manhood real, but it was also perfect. Jesus was the only man in history who could confidently ask, 'Which of you convicts me of sin? And if I tell the truth, why do you not believe me?' (John 8:46). The innocence of his character was witnessed to by even Pilate, the one who ordered his execution (John 18:38) and Judas who betrayed him (Matt. 27:4). The lamb that was to be slain for the Passover was to be a male of the first year, 'without blemish' (Exod. 12:5). Jesus, the one ordained of God to be the Lamb slain for the sin of the world, was 'holy, harmless, undefiled, separate from sinners' (Heb. 7:26).

Jesus was a perfect man

1. *His holiness was original.* Jesus Christ was not born with a sinful nature like the rest of humanity because he was supernaturally conceived in the womb of his mother Mary (Isa. 7:14; Matt. 1:23; Luke 1:27). The foetus of Jesus was miraculously created by the Holy Spirit in union with Mary's body. Having no earthly father Jesus Christ had no original sin. That which is created by God cannot be anything but perfect.

2. *His holiness was actual.* Speaking of the Messiah, the prophet Isaiah said, 'The LORD is well pleased for his righteousness' sake; he will exalt the law and make it honourable' (42:21). Jesus Christ came under the law because of his real manhood. Since he was a Jew he grew up obeying the sanctions of the Mosaic system, which he as the Messiah was to abolish. He was acknowledged as the 'Son of David' (Matt. 12:23). His genealogical line connected him with Abraham through David (see Matt. 1).

Like all Jewish boys Jesus was circumcized on the eighth day and his mother Mary underwent the customary purification rites (Luke 2:21-24). His parents honoured the Jewish festivities, such as the Passover (Luke 2:41). When Jesus began his public ministry he first spoke in the local synagogue, where the Old Testament Scriptures were expounded weekly. As far as it was according to the original intention of the Mosaic law, he honoured the Sabbath day. He did not, however, bind himself to the superstitious additions of the Jewish doctors, whose followers in Jesus' day were the Scribes and Pharisees.

Jesus was present at the temple when the Feast of Tabernacles was observed (John 7:14). John 10:22 mentions that Jesus was at the 'winter' Feast of Dedication, which is thought to have been the celebration inaugurated by the Jews following the restoration of the temple after its desecration by Antiochus Epiphanes.

More importantly, the life of Jesus showed a flawless obedience to every demand of God's moral law, which is summed up in love to God and man, and codified in a way especially adaptable to Israel, in the Ten Commandments.

Characteristics of Jesus' holiness

1. *It was complete.* The will of God touches both the outward life and the inward attitude as well (Ps. 51:6; Jer. 31:33). There is no record of Jesus violating the commands of God in the smallest detail. He loved God with all his heart and always showed pity, compassion and mercy towards his fellow men. The goodness of ordinary men is often only outward, but not so with Christ. His holiness was rooted in a sinless nature.

2. *It was balanced.* It is a common frailty of ordinary men to be good or righteous in one area of responsibility but negligent in others. One man will be honest but will curse and drink. Another will be kind to his family but has no scruples about stealing. Even the saints of God are, as a rule, unbalanced to some degree. One will be taken up with the glory of God and worship him, but have a tendency towards being rude and thoughtless towards other people. Another will be generous and benevolent with his fellow men, but will neglect basic duties of church attendance, Bible reading and prayer. Not so with Jesus. He was both a worshipper and a worker. The Scriptures often call our attention to the times when

Jesus drew aside for seasons of prayer (Matt. 14:23; Mark 6:46). When confronted by Satan with a temptation to turn aside from his mission of self-denial and service to God, he steadfastly resisted saying, 'Get behind me, Satan!' (Luke 4:8).

Jesus' life was an unbroken course of service to those about him. Luke sums this up in short by saying that Jesus 'went about doing good' (Acts 10:38). He not only felt sympathy for his neighbours and countrymen but set about putting these feelings into practice. He healed the sick and comforted them. He wept with those who wept (John 11:35). He constantly sought the physical, emotional and spiritual well-being not just of his own body and soul but those of others.

Consider the various relationships of men and how Jesus showed perfect, balanced virtue in all of them, to the extent of his involvement with other people.

a. *Domestic.* Jesus was in subjection to his parents (Luke 2:51). He provided for the care of his mother while dying on the cross (John 19:26-27).
b. *Civic.* Jesus showed respect to the reigning government of Rome and encouraged his disciples to pay taxes dutifully (Matt. 22:21).
c. *Social.* Although Jesus was personally very poor, having virtually no personal possessions, his disciples carried a purse from which donations were made to the poor (John 12:6). Jesus taught generosity and compassion to his disciples (Matt. 5:42; Luke 10:30-37).
d. *Spiritual.* Jesus worshipped and served God, and honoured the divinely established religious system of his day (Matt. 26:55).

In summary, we can see that in all areas of life Jesus was faithful to God and taught his disciples the same pattern of living.

3. *Jesus' obedience was unvaried and consistent.* As the old Puritans used to say, even the most godly men are prone to serve God by 'fits and starts'; that is, they run hot and cold. There are times when they burn with zeal, but at other times they are prone to apathy and lukewarmness. There are periods of faithfulness and fervency in prayer, but also times of negligence.

But Jesus' life was a uniform and uninterrupted course of holiness. Even when a twelve-year-old youth he said, 'I must be about my Father's business' (Luke 2:49). Twenty-one years later, when facing the agony of Calvary to which the Father had destined him, he resigned his own will to that of God's (Luke 22:42). This was true also in the intervening years.

4. *Jesus' life of service and obedience was sincere.* The law of God requires a genuine, honest and pure love to God, and a life of sincere service, as opposed to guile and hypocrisy (Josh. 24:14). Men are notoriously prone to mere outward service, even when their obedience is not properly motivated and genuine. But the Son of God was free from deceit (1 Peter 2:22).

Jesus was the God-man

Jesus Christ was one person with two natures, a divine nature and a human nature. The divine nature of Christ was veiled but not diminished by its union with the manhood of Jesus. The human nature was exalted but not absorbed by its union with the divine. The 'ego' of Christ was that of one self-consciousness, that is, he was one personality. It was the personality of the second person of the Trinity in union with human nature. It was not the Father that assumed human nature, nor that of the Holy Spirit, but the nature of the Son. The Son was made in the likeness of sinful flesh (Rom. 8:3;

Phil. 2:7) and 'dwelt among us' (John 1:14). The Greek
word for 'dwelt' is *skenoo*, which means to 'camp in a tent',
alluding perhaps to the fact that the Old Testament tabernacle, which was a tent, was a type of Jesus who 'dwelt' or
'tabernacled' among men.

The union of the two natures of Christ in one personality
is too much for the human mind to comprehend. Paul called
it the 'mystery of godliness' (1 Tim. 3:16). The believer does
not question, but in adoring wonder praises God for a Saviour
who is *God and man.*

New Testament teachings on Christ as Redeemer

The New Testament sets out the complete revelation of God
about his Son, the Redeemer of man. Jesus is declared to be
God, man and the God-man. There are certain works that
Jesus accomplished which could be attributed only to his
divine nature, such as creation. There are some things he did
which could be attributed only to his human nature, such as
sleeping and eating. But those works that Jesus performed
that pertain directly to the salvation of sinners, he did in his
capacity as the God-man. The uniqueness of his complex
personality made his work as Saviour or Mediator possible.

Christ's mediatorial work is in three offices

A proper understanding of the work of Christ as Saviour must
take into account the three offices of Jesus Christ. All of these
have roots in the Old Testament, which prepared the way,
typically, for the Messianic period.

1. *Jesus Christ was the supreme Prophet* (Luke 13:33; Acts
3:22). The prophetic office was ordinarily fulfilled in three

ways: teaching, foretelling the future and miracle working. Christ participated in all of these things. But not only did he proclaim truth through verbal instruction, he also revealed the Father through his person, life and work. John 1:18 states that no one has seen God the Father but the Son has 'declared' him. In all that Jesus was, he set forth the nature of God. One of his names is the Word of God (John 1:1). A word is an expression of thought, a communication. Jesus is the supreme revelation, expression and communication about God.

2. *Jesus Christ was the supreme Priest.* The priestly office was established by God in the Mosaic dispensation, although we do find a mention of an ancient priest named Melchizedek earlier in the book of Genesis (Gen. 14:18-20). A priest was a person ordained of God to transact with God on behalf of man.

3. *Jesus Christ is King.* How Christ functions as Lord and King will be explained later.

Saviour from sin

It is in his office as a priest that Jesus officiates as a Saviour from sin. He did this in two ways. Firstly, by making a sacrifice for sin, which he did when he died on the cross; and secondly, by making intercession, which is a part of Christ's ongoing ministry in heaven.

Atonement for sinners

When Jesus died on a Roman cross outside Jerusalem, he made an atonement for sinners. In the Old Testament Scriptures, it was stated that one who was hanged on a tree was cursed (Deut. 21:23). Paul cites the crucifixion of Christ as the supreme fulfilment of this. He was cursed for those for whom he died (Gal. 3:13).

Infinite sin demands infinite penalty

When dealing with the subject of sin we showed that man's guilt caused him to lose the favour of God. There is no fitting penalty for man's sin but eternal separation from God. Because Jesus Christ was God, he was able in a few hours to swallow up, as it were, the infinite wrath of God against his people. No measure or limit can be placed on the guilt of sinners, and no measure or limit can be placed on the value of Christ's blood.

Key words that explain Christ's priestly work

1. *Imputation.* The Bible speaks both of the imputing of sin (Rom. 4:8) and righteousness (Rom. 4:6). While the Bible does not state explicitly that sin was imputed to Christ it uses expressions that cannot possibly be interpreted in any other way. Isaiah 53:6 states that the iniquity of us all was laid on him. 2 Corinthians 5:21 says that God made Christ to be sin for us, although he personally knew no sin.

a. *The difference between imputation and infusion.* Sin did not become a part of Christ's person or essence as he died on the cross. Imputation means that Jesus bore the guilt of sin, that is, he bore the death demanded by the law for the sinner: spiritual death, as well as physical death. In human legal transactions moral debts cannot be transferred, but in the counsels of heaven God 'found a way' to rid the sinner of guilt, and that is by imputation. As John 1:29 says, Jesus 'takes away' the sin of the world.

b. *The ground of imputation.* Jesus Christ was perfectly
innocent in his actual life and character. So on what ground
could God charge the sins of men upon his Son? The
answer seems to lie in the words *union* and *identification,*
although it is essential that we exercise caution here because the Bible does not answer this question categorically.
Just as Adam was the organic head of the human race,
Christ united himself to human nature and became the
Head of a new race of believers in union with him. Hebrews
2:16 says that he did not take upon himself the nature of
angels but the nature of the seed of Abraham. Even if we
could not explain the 'why' of Christ's identification with
sinners, still we must accept it as a fact. If there would be
any suspicion of unjustness about Christ's incarnation and
substitutionary death, let us remember that Jesus voluntarily assumed human nature and agreed to be man's
Saviour (John 10:18).

2. *Righteousness.* The phrase 'righteousness of God' is often
used in the New Testament (Rom. 1:17; 3:21-22; 2 Cor. 5:21).
It is used in connection with the priestly work of Christ in
dying for our sins, and seems to convey two ideas: firstly, the
righteousness which God requires; and secondly, the righteousness which God provides.

God requires perfect righteousness for fellowship with
him. Nothing less would suit his divine purity. Again, there is
no adequate penalty for failure to measure up to these demands except eternal separation from God (Rom. 6:23). By
his life and death Jesus Christ supplied, through the grace
and purpose of God, a righteousness that fully meets God's
requirements. By his life he established a righteousness
which can be credited to believers, and by his death he took
away the cause of the offence to God: sin. Thus believers are
made free from the penalty of sin (Rom. 8:3-4) and are

righteous in Christ (Phil. 3:9). Jesus is our righteousness (1 Cor. 1:30).

3. *Propitiation* (Rom. 3:25; 1 John 2:2). The central idea of propitiation is to appease. This aspect of Christ's work views God as displeased, even angry, with man for his sin (Rom. 1:18). The death of Christ on behalf of sinners satisfied, appeased, placated the righteous God and turned away his indignation against those who are in Christ. This word is very important, for it shows that the atonement is primarily God-ward, not man-ward. Just as the offerings of the Old Testament gave a sweet smell when mingled with incense, so the death of Christ was a sweet-smelling aroma to God (Eph. 5:2).

4. *Reconciliation* (Eph. 2:16; 2 Cor. 5:19).

a. *Meaning of reconciliation.* The word *reconcile* stresses the changed relationship the believing sinner has with God as a result of the death of Christ. Because of the Fall, man is an enemy of God (Rom. 5:10) and is alienated from him (Eph. 2:12). The atonement removes the cause of this alienation because the sin debt is satisfied. Since God is 'propitiated' man is reconciled, that is, restored to a position of fellowship. After the believing sinner is thus brought back into a relationship with Christ, Christ is his 'peace' (Eph. 2:14).

b. *Provisional and actual reconciliation.* Does the actual reconciliation of the sinner take place when Christ died or does it take place when one becomes a believer? On the surface there is a problem with either position. If we say that actual reconciliation was at Calvary, then faith is not essential to a right relationship to God, but is only a 'discovery' of what is already a fact. But the Bible says the wrath of God is upon all unbelievers, even though the events of the cross have happened (John 3:36). Yet such texts as 2 Corinthians 5:19 seem to imply that reconciliation took place the moment Christ died. Does faith 'add' to the reconciliation of Christ? Would not answering 'yes' to this question dishonour the perfect sacrifice of Christ? The fact seems to be that at the cross all that was necessary for the satisfaction of the law was accomplished. Faith adds nothing to that. But one must be in union with Christ through faith to receive the benefit of it.

5. *Redemption.* There is no more meaningful word to describe the work of Christ for his people than redemption. There are three words used for redemption in the New Testament. One is *agorazo,* which means to buy at the market place, as for example in Revelation 5:9. Another word is *exagorazo,* which means to buy out of the market place, as used in Galatians 3:13. Both of these words suggest the payment of a price (1 Cor. 6:20). The price was the blood of Jesus Christ, a payment of infinite merit and value. This price was paid not to Satan but to the justice of God.

The third word is *lutroo,* which means to 'lose or free' by the payment of a price (Titus 2:14; 1 Peter 1:18). The price is called a 'ransom' (1 Tim. 2:6; Matt. 20:28). Here the idea of a 'deliverance' is strong.

The concept of redemption is a familiar one in the Old Testament. For example, if a man through poverty had to sell himself as a slave, one of his kin could 'redeem' him or buy his freedom (Lev. 25:47-49). Through sin we were sold to a stranger, Satan, which brought us under bondage to the curse of the law. Jesus' blood was the price that secured our freedom.

6. *Justification.* The word justify is a legal term which means to 'declare righteous'. It has reference to a court-room

procedure when the judge pronounces the accused 'free from blame'. The New Testament Scriptures teach that the believer has been justified before God or freed from all charge of guilt (Rom. 3:28; Gal. 2:16).

Justification differs from forgiveness in two respects. First, it is *once and for all* and has reference to a permanent relationship to the law. The believer is justified once and for all. But forgiveness can be repeated many times and relates to the believer's walk. The second difference is the way the believer is viewed. In justification he is viewed as righteous in Christ; in forgiveness he is viewed in his actual condition as a sinner, needing God's mercy.

The grace of God is the cause of justification (Rom. 3:24). The redemption of Christ is the basis of justification (Rom. 3:24). Faith is the instrument (Rom. 3:28). Good works have nothing to do with our acceptance with God, but manifest or evidence our salvation, thus we are justified outwardly by works (James 2:24).

7. *Sanctification.* The root meaning of sanctify is to set apart. There is a sense in which the saved are 'set apart' or consecrated to God by the blood of Christ (Heb. 10:14). This is a legal or objective sanctification. Subjective sanctification through the Holy Spirit takes place at regeneration and gradually progresses.

The two-fold reference of the atonement

There are certain verses of Scripture that attribute universality to the death of Christ (John 1:29; 2 Cor. 5:19; 1 Tim. 2:6; 1 John 2:2). There are others which teach just as plainly that it is designed specially for the people of God (Matt. 20:28; John 10:15; Rom. 8:32; Eph. 5:25). When the whole scope of the satisfaction of Christ is taken into consideration we can see that there is no contradiction in the two aspects of his work.

The so-called 'universal' verses show what the work of Christ is sufficient for and adapted for. In the cross there is a potential provision for the salvation of all men of all times and nations. The fact that all are invited to Christ confirms this fact. No one will go to hell for the lack of atonement. Christ would not have needed to obey the law any more perfectly or suffered more if the whole world were to accept him.

But this is not the whole truth. Whether the atonement of Christ succeeds or not (whether any are saved by it) is not, in the final analysis, left to the choices of men. Although the gospel is freely offered to all, and God desires that all turn to him (1 Tim. 2:4), the salvation of a certain number of people is secured by the sovereign will of God as exercised in the covenant of redemption. This purpose in the Bible is called 'election'.

The covenant of redemption

A covenant is an arrangement whereby two or more parties enter into an agreement in which each is bound to do certain things, depending on the nature of the covenant. It can involve promises, and rewards or penalties on the part of the parties engaged in it. Adam entered into an arrangement or covenant with God, in which there were conditions to be met on Adam's part, and promises or warnings on God's part. The warning was that if he sinned by eating the forbidden fruit he would die. Implied was the fact that he would live if he obeyed. When Adam sinned he broke the covenant (Hosea 6:7). The word for men here is literally 'Adam'.

In Isaiah 42:6 we read that God said to his Son, 'I will keep you and give you as a covenant to the people.' In other words, Jesus Christ's coming into the world was a part of an arrangement or agreement between him and the Father. On many occasions Jesus referred to the fact that he was sent into the world by the Father (John 5:37) and that he came to earth voluntarily to do God's will (John 6:38). This amounts to a covenant between two parties. There were promises made to the Son based on the condition of his faithfulness to the Father in becoming incarnate and a substitute for sinners. One promise was that God would sustain him in the arduous undertaking of being a Saviour of men (Isa. 42:6). The Father also promised to exalt him to a position of glory and honour (Ps. 16:10; 110:1).

God promised Christ that there would be a definite number of people given to him who would be saved by the application of his redemption (John 6:37; 6:39; 17:2). The gift of a people to Christ involves the doctrine of election. The following points are pertinent.

The doctrine of election

1. Election was from eternity (Eph. 1:4; 2 Thess. 2:13).
2. Election is the carrying out of God's sovereign good pleasure (Rom. 9:11).
3. Election is personal (Rom. 16:13).
4. Election is unto salvation (2 Thess. 2:13).
5. Election is gracious, that is, it is rooted in the love and mercy of God towards sinners, and is not a reward for foreseen merit or action on man's part (Rom. 11:5-7).
6. Election is according to God's foreknowledge (1 Peter 1:2). God knew his people ahead of time. He knew they would never choose or come to him apart from his sovereign grace.
7. Election is in Christ (Eph. 1:4). From all eternity Christ was the seminal head or fountain of life to his people. God viewed his people as related to Christ, in his purpose to save them.
8. Election includes all the means to bring about the salvation of the elect, which involves predestination. All who are elected

will be called by the gospel and will believe the truth. They *will* come to Christ, because they *must* come to Christ.

a. *Election and predestination.* The word predestination is mentioned four times in the New Testament (Eph. 1:5, 11; Rom. 8:29-30). It is the effective carrying out in time of God's eternal decree to bring men to himself. It brings means to bear on the end.

b. *Election and effectual atonement.* The work of Christ on the cross was the greatest of all God's works. It is the climax of his plan for the human race. It is unreasonable, certainly it is unscriptural, to suppose that this might fail. The covenant of redemption guarantees the deliverance of the church through the sacrifice of Christ. As Isaiah 53:11 says, 'He shall see the labour of his soul, and be satisfied. By his knowledge my righteous Servant shall justify many, for he shall bear their iniquities.' Jesus said, 'And other sheep I have which are not of this fold; them also I must bring, and they will hear my voice; and there will be one flock and one shepherd' (John 10:16).

God's acceptance of Christ's sacrifice

The sixth of Christ's sayings on the cross was 'It is finished.' How do we know that Christ finished his work of atonement for man, and how do we know that God accepted this sacrifice? A. W. Pink points out four ways we can know this. First, the rending of the veil, which showed that the way to God was now open. Second, in the raising of Christ from the dead. Third, in the exaltation of Christ and his enthronement at God's right hand. Fourth, the sending of the Holy Spirit to earth to apply Christ's death.[8]

The resurrection of Christ

The gospel is not simply a declaration of the fact that Jesus Christ died for our sins on the cross. It also includes the fact that he was buried and rose again (1 Cor. 15:1-4). All four Gospels give an account of Christ's burial and resurrection. He appeared to his disciples in bodily form and even ate with them (John 21:12-13).

1. *The fact of the resurrection.* The proof of the resurrection lies in the fact that it was reported by reliable witnesses. They saw him, talked to him and even felt him (John 20:27-28). This means that his resurrection was literal and physical. His body and soul were reunited. Although Jesus' body was sinless before his death, it was subject to limitations and weaknesses. But after the resurrection his body, though real and material, seemed to be above such limitations. He was not easily recognized and he suddenly appeared and disappeared in a surprising manner (Luke 24:36-39).

2. *The author of the resurrection.* The resurrection of Christ was by the power of the triune God. The Father raised him from the dead (Gal. 1:1). Jesus stated that he himself had the power to lay down his life and take it again (John 10:18). But his human nature was also quickened by the Spirit (1 Peter 3:18). Like all the works of God, the resurrection was according to the purpose of the Father, the authority of the Son, and the agency of the Spirit.

3. *The results of the resurrection*

a. Christ's claims, including that of being the Son of God, were vindicated (Rom. 1:4).

b. Christ became a 'quickening Spirit' or source of life for all
his people (1 Cor. 15:45). The first Adam died and brought
death. Jesus Christ, the second Adam, rose and brought
life. His resurrection was a pledge of the resurrection of
all believers (1 Cor. 15:20-23). Christ is called 'the firstfruits
of those who have fallen asleep'. The firstfruits were the
first part of the grain that sprang out of the earth. It was
soonest ripe and first reaped and gathered in. So Christ
rose not as a private individual but as the Head and
Representative of his people. In baptism, the believer is
identified with Christ in his death, burial and resurrection
(Rom. 6:3-5).

c. Christ's resurrection secured the justification of believers
(Rom. 4:25). When Christ came out from the grave, it was
a sign that sin had been put away. Hebrews 1:3 says that
after Jesus had 'purged our sins', he 'sat down at the right
hand of the majesty on high'. It is a living Saviour to which
men turn for justification through faith.

5.
Learning about the experience of grace

Although the gospel centres primarily around the historical fact of the death, burial and resurrection of Christ, it does not stop there. The whole scope of the gospel takes into account not only what Christ *did* for sinners, but what he *is doing*. The ministry of Christ continues because he not only rose again but also ascended into heaven and sat down at the right hand of the Father to rule and reign. It is in this position of authority and glory that Jesus *applies* the merits of his redemption. Thus we have the experiential aspect of salvation, or the application of salvation in the life of the believer.

The exaltation of Christ

A major New Testament theme

The enthronement of Christ at the right hand of God is a major New Testament theme. In his message on Pentecost Peter, after relating the facts concerning Christ's earthly ministry and death, launches into the subject, taking his texts from Psalm 16 and Psalm 110. In the former it is stated that

God would not suffer his Holy One to see corruption, and
that his soul was not left in 'Hades'. Peter says that this refers
to the resurrection of Christ (Acts 2:31).

Among the numerous other passages which bring out the
exaltation and sovereignty of Christ are Acts 5:31; Ephesians
1:19-22; Hebrews 1:3; 10:12-13; and 1 Peter 3:22. One of the
fullest statements is Philippians 2:9-12.

Jesus' ascension authority

Jesus received authority to govern and rule by his ascension.
At that time he entered into a position of glory, exaltation
and authority. The authority with which Jesus was invested
is the key to understanding the kingdom of God and God's
programme for this age and the future. Even during the time
of his earthly ministry, during which he experienced suffering and humiliation, Christ frequently affirmed his sense of
mission to rule over all men and nations. Just before he
washed the disciples' feet it is said he knew 'that the Father
had given all things into his hands' (John 13:3). On another
occasion Jesus said, 'For the Father judges no one, but has
committed all judgement to the Son' (John 5:22). The word
'judge' has a narrow meaning: to adjudicate for the last time
at the final day of reckoning. But it has also a broader meaning: to rule or govern, the former meaning being included in
the latter. The meaning here in John 5 has the larger scope.
To cite another place where Jesus alluded to this authority,
in Matthew 28:18 we read, 'And Jesus came and spoke to
them, saying, "All authority has been given to me in heaven
and on earth."'

The foregoing passages of Scripture establish one of the
basic truths of the New Testament relating to God's government of the universe; namely, that all affairs are now under

the sovereign jurisdiction of Jesus Christ, the incarnate Son. As Dr John Brown states, 'The Father does not directly, but by the Son administer government under the new economy; he hath committed all government to the Son.'[9]

The *universality* of the authority of Christ is worthy of note. Not only are all things created by Christ, but all things are under his dominion and government. 1 Peter 3:22 makes it clear that this includes angels as well as men. Even the demon spirits or fallen angels recognized the power of Christ over them (Matt. 8:29; Mark 1:24).

The kingdom of Jesus

Jesus has established a kingdom under the exercise of his sovereign authority. When we have a clear grasp of the truth that God governs the world through the Son, then we have a foundation for definite, scriptural views on the 'kingdom of God' and 'kingdom of Christ'. The kingdom of God is nothing more than his sovereign rule through Jesus Christ. This rule comprehends the entire creation or universe. Obviously believers on earth are a part of a material universe and thus they are affected by all the processes of the natural world. They are on a globe that rotates and circles the sun. They are pulled by the gravitation of the earth, they eat food that needs the nourishment of the soil and rain, and their bodies are invaded by hostile viruses and germs. Political and social changes redirect their lives and careers. The authority of Christ's kingdom and his administrative rule over time and space must necessarily extend to these realms.

Colossians 1:17 states that by him all things 'consist' or hold together. Ephesians 1:22 says that God has put all things under the feet of Christ and that he is Head 'over all things' to the church. Tying these passages together we get the picture of Jesus Christ sitting on the throne of the universe 'managing' all the movements of the interplanetary and stellar systems, the intricate balances of planet earth and the events of history.

But the authority of Christ over the universe is only the *external* aspect of his rule. There is an *internal* and spiritual aspect to his dominion in the hearts of those who believe in him. The following references establish this point.

On one occasion the Pharisees came to Jesus and asked when the kingdom would come. His answer was that the kingdom does not come with observation, but is 'within you' (Luke 17:20-21). Literally this means 'in your midst'. When Jesus the King and his people were among these people the kingdom had come. This refers obviously to Christ's present, spiritual kingdom.

Jesus said that the kingdom is entered by the new birth (John 3:3, 5) or, from the human side, conversion (Matt. 18:3-4). He also said that the kingdom consists of those who are 'poor in spirit' (Matt. 5:3).

Paul refers to the great deliverance of men from an unconverted state in these terms: 'He has delivered us from the power of darkness and conveyed us into the kingdom of the Son of his love' (Col. 1:13).

These verses indicate that there is a kingdom of God, which includes only a portion of the human race. These are those who acknowledge Christ as their Lord and have submitted to his rule over them. Christ's sovereign authority over his people is one of his functions as a King. As a Prophet he teaches his church, as a Priest he atoned for their sins and intercedes for them, and as a King he rules over them and protects them. Jesus rules over all men through his providence; those who actually submit to him are his willing subjects.

Man's response to the gospel: conversion

Christ's exaltation places all mankind under obligation

Shortly before his ascension into heaven Jesus commissioned his disciples to go into the world and proclaim his gospel or the good news. His command, 'Go preach — go make disciples' is based on his sovereign authority (Matt. 28:17-20). This suggests that Christ's substitutionary death and triumphant resurrection laid the foundation for a great opportunity for man to be saved. It is the mission of the church to take the gospel to sinners so they can have this opportunity.

But if the saving work of Christ on Calvary and his enthronement at the right hand of God provides an opportunity for men, it also puts them under obligation. This obligation, in short, is that all who hear the message *respond* in the proper way.

If Christ has died on the cross and freely offers his grace and mercy to men, then people who hear the message are to turn from their sins and receive the message, in other words, repent and believe.

If Christ has risen triumphant over death, ascended into heaven where he is enthroned at the right hand of God, then all should submit.

Repentance, faith and submission all imply each other. A person cannot repent without believing and submitting; he cannot believe without repenting and submitting; and he cannot submit without repenting and believing. In fact, *believing* is used sometimes in Scripture to encompass the whole act of the soul in embracing Christ, including repentance and submission. Jesus' invitation for men to come to him and take his yoke is an invitation to salvation (Matt. 11:28-29). A yoke is a symbol of submission. Also, 2

Thessalonians 1:8 says that when Christ comes he will take vengeance on those who do not 'obey' the gospel. To obey is to submit.

However, the emphasis of the New Testament is on faith as terminating or fixing on Christ as the sacrifice for sin. The sinner is conscious of a need for forgiveness and looking at the crucified Saviour he finds forgiveness and relief from the burden of sin. We will now consider faith as the act of receiving Christ as Saviour.

Faith: its necessity and nature

The distinguishing mark of those who are in the kingdom of Christ is believing. No man can please God without faith (Heb. 11:6). Also, no man can be saved without it (John 3:16; Eph. 2:8-9). He who comes to God must believe that he is (Heb. 11:6). Since faith is required of all who hear the gospel and brings one into a state of salvation it is important that we understand the nature of saving faith. Essentially there are three elements in faith. These are intellectual acceptance, trust and submission.

1. *Intellectual acceptance.* Faith is always based on fact, or what is deemed to be fact, whether we are dealing in the natural or the spiritual world. For example, we consider it a fact that a man named Christopher Columbus was commissioned by Spanish royalty to cross the Atlantic and seek fame and fortune for his homeland. Though we have never seen the man, we accept the testimony of history about him. We believe in the credibility of history.

In the Bible there are certain things revealed which faith accepts as factual. Some of these facts deal with natural historical events, such as the truth that Cain killed his brother

Abel. Others pertain to the gospel and deal with things that are not normal in the natural order. Faith accepts the testimony of God that such supernatural events as creation and the miracles of Jesus actually occurred. We were not there when God created the world any more than we were there when Columbus landed on the coast of San Salvador, but we believe in these facts based on credible history.

Faith especially believes what the Bible says about the person and work of Christ. It accepts the fact that he was born of a virgin, lived a perfect life, died for sinners and rose again from the dead. Faith recognizes that the Bible teaches that Christ was both God and man, that he existed eternally with the Father before coming to earth, that he lived a perfect life on earth, died for sin and was raised from the dead. When a person believes this with his whole heart (Acts 8:37; 16:30-31), he becomes a Christian. There are many parts of the Bible the believer does not understand. There are truths of Scripture that overwhelm him with their weight and glory. But even when human reason cannot plumb the depths of the truths of God, faith says, 'Lord, I believe; help my unbelief!' (Mark 9:24).

2. *Trust.* If we really believe in an object of strength and sufficiency we can readily commit ourselves to it. Faith is a principle of life we cannot live without. We depend on things every day because we have confidence in them. We purchase equipment, vehicles and appliances because we believe in the trustworthiness of their manufacturers and dealers. We eat food because we believe in the competency of those preparing it. We deposit our money in banks, submit our bodies to surgeons and pay premiums to insurance companies to protect us from cataclysmic loss. Even the simple acts of seeing or hearing involves trust, because we must believe in

the validity of our own faculties. We believe that the image focused inside the eye and transferred to the brain is an accurate picture of the scene before us.

In the spiritual realm we find the supreme application of these facts. God is set forth in Scripture as an all-sufficient, omnipotent source of trust for his creatures. God's Son is proclaimed in the gospel as the one who made perfect satisfaction to the justice of God for our sins. He invites sinners to come and find refuge in him.

When a person believes the gospel report or accepts in his heart the gospel testimony concerning Christ, he will in that act lay hold upon him personally and trust him for salvation. The elements of saving trust in Christ are found in 2 Timothy 1:12: 'For I know whom I have believed and am persuaded that he is able to keep what I have committed to him until that day.' Paul committed his life to the Lord Jesus Christ; and in particular, the eternal welfare of his soul. Notice that Paul's commitment was made to the one whom he believed, and that this belief produced a persuasion in his mind that impelled him to trust.

3. *Submission.* The gospel proclaims Jesus Christ not only as Saviour but also as Lord (Acts 16:31). To be converted means to acknowledge this Lordship and submit to the Lord personally (Rom. 10:9). The act of trusting in God and in his Son through the gospel is more than an act of the mind. It is also an act of the affections and will. It involves resigning the thoughts and deeds of the flesh. To respond positively to the Lord Jesus Christ means to kiss him in surrender (Ps. 2:12), take his yoke and learn of him (Matt. 11:29) and obey him (Heb. 5:9). The faith that saves manifests itself in continuance in the faith (Col. 1:23) and good works (James 2:20).

Pictures of faith

In order to help us to understand the nature of saving faith God has given a number of word pictures to describe it.

1. *Looking to Christ.* The primary function of the physical eye is to see objects in the world around us. When the soul is enabled to behold the sufficiency of God and look to him spiritually, it is called looking. 'Look to me, and be saved, all you ends of the earth! For I am God, and there is no other' (Isa. 45:22). The classic illustration of looking to God for salvation is seen in the story of the brazen serpent that God provided for the Israelites (Num. 21:8-9). The people had been bitten by poisonous serpents, but all who looked to the serpent of brass were healed. Jesus applies this to faith (John 3:14-15).

2. *Running to Christ for refuge.* In the Old Testament a provision was made to protect those who had killed without malicious intent. Cities of refuge were placed at convenient locations so that the slayer could run and be saved from the avenger who was seeking to kill him (Num. 35:6-15). This is a picture of the sinner running to Christ from the avenging power of the law of God. Hebrews 6:18 says that believers 'have fled for refuge to lay hold of the hope set before us'.

3. *Coming to Christ.* The word 'come' has a warm and friendly sound to it. In the gospel God invites sinners to 'come to the feast' that he has spread: the provision of salvation. The king who sent out an invitation for his friends to come to the wedding feast illustrates the gospel proclamation. 'All things are ready. Come to the wedding' (Matt. 22:4). The same idea can be seen in Matthew 11:28 and Revelation 22:17.

Accompanying this invitation is the golden promise of John 6:37: 'the one who comes to me I will by no means cast out'.

4. *Eating and drinking*. God is represented in the Bible as the source of all good and pleasure (Ps. 16:11). Christ taught his disciples that he was the bread of life (John 6:35), the antitype of the manna that God sent from heaven to feed the Israelites. Just as bread nourishes the body, so partaking of Christ by faith brings eternal life (John 6:56). Also, Jesus invites those who are spiritually thirsty to come to him and drink (John 7:37), thus reminding us that he is the 'fountain of living water' (see also Rev. 22:17).

Such terms as 'the new birth', 'conversion', 'faith' and 're-pentance' are all used with reference to the mighty change that takes place when a person becomes a Christian. The new birth views this change as a transformation of nature, brought about by the sovereign power of God. It is the sinner's deliverance from God's standpoint. Conversion looks at it from man's standpoint. Conversion means 'turning' and is required of men if they would go to heaven (Matt. 18:3; Acts 3:19). When a person is saved he turns around, changes his direction of travel, as it were. Conversion has two sides: the positive side (which we have been discussing), and the nega-tive side, repentance. They go hand in hand. One cannot believe without repenting any more than a person can go into a house without leaving the outside, or turn to the right with-out leaving the left.

Repentance

Repentance is one of the conditions of salvation, or one of the terms required for men to enter the kingdom of God. Repentance was preached by the New Testament heralds of salvation. This is true of John the Baptist (Matt. 3:2), Jesus (Luke 13:3), Peter (Acts 2:38), and Paul (Acts 26:20). Repentance is the voluntary change of mind in the sinner by which he turns from sin to God. The mind, the heart and the will are all involved in it.

There is an intellectual element, for the penitent sees and acknowledges his sin (Ps. 51:3, 7, 9). There is an emotional element, for the penitent feels sorrow for his sin, not just because of its consequences but because he has offended God (2 Cor. 7:9-11). There is a voluntary element for the penitent turns from sin and seeks cleansing and pardon (Prov. 28:13; Ps. 51:7, 10; 1 Thess. 1:9).

Results of faith

1. *Justification.* One of the greatest questions any person can ask was posed by Bildad in the ancient days of Job: 'How then can man be righteous before God? Or how can he be pure who is born of a woman?'(Job 25:4). This question is answered in type and by implication in the Old Testament and by historical fulfilment and direct explanation in the New Testament. God, moved only by his own merciful nature, through the redemption of Christ, justifies the believing sinner. The moment a person believes in Christ personally, he is declared righteous and thus accepted in God's sight (John 3:17; 5:24; Rom. 5:1).

Faith is not the cause or ground of justification but the instrument of justification. Grace is the cause of justification (Titus 3:7), the blood of Christ is the meritorious ground (Rom. 5:9) and faith is the instrument (Rom. 3:28).

2. *Adoption.* It is through faith that we can become the sons of God (John 1:12; Gal. 3:26). Ephesians 1:5 affirms that 'adoption as sons' is one of the ends of God's predestination.

In some ways, God's adoption of his people is like the civil adoptions in earthly relationships. A couple with no natural children, through a civil procedure that is often long and tedious, can become the legal parents of a child or children born to others. These adopted children become full members of the family with all the rights of this relationship.

In human adoptions, however, the children still have the genetic connection with those who bore them. They will always have the physical features and personality derived from their natural parents. But when God adopts lost sinners into his family, he gives them his own nature. They are recreated in his image.

There are many privileges that the adopted sons of God have. They have the 'spirit of adoption' in their hearts, that is, the assurance that God is their Father (Rom. 8:15). They have direct access through the blood of Jesus into the presence of God and intimate fellowship with their heavenly Father (Eph. 2:13). They are heirs of God and joint heirs with Jesus Christ of all the blessings of heaven (Rom. 8:17; Eph. 1:11; 1 Peter 1:4).

Regeneration

Conversion is the human side of the experience of grace; regeneration is the divine side. Theologically, regeneration should precede our study of conversion since God's work precedes man's. But we have been looking at salvation as it comes to us — in response to the gospel offer; thus the human side of salvation was considered first.

Definition of regeneration

Regeneration is a work of God whereby he implants in man's moral nature a holy principle that produces obedience to God.

It is more than outward reformation or adherence to the forms of worship or the ordinances of the church. The nature of this change is both difficult to understand and mysterious because the human personality is itself a mystery. Also, the way the Holy Spirit works is beyond human comprehension.

The necessity of regeneration

The Bible teaches and human experience confirms the fact that human nature is in need of this change. Like the broken mainspring of a watch, there is something wrong at the very base of man's being. We cite three obvious reasons as to why the new birth is necessary, although this certainly does not exhaust the subject.

1. Holiness is essential to fellowship with God, and man is a sinner devoid of holiness (Isa. 59:2).

2. Heaven could not be appreciated or enjoyed apart from a nature in love with God. The truth is that if an unsaved man would go to heaven he would run to hell for refuge.

3. Holiness is the end of man and he cannot be complete or happy without a right relationship with God. Apart from God man is like an engine out of tune. Regeneration sets the life of the sinner on the right course.

The Author of regeneration

God alone can produce a new nature in the soul of fallen man. This is seen in the following facts.

1. *Man is unable to regenerate himself.* Because of his spiritual blindness, love of sin, and voluntary rejection of truth, the sinner will not turn to God (Jer. 13:23). Job asked: 'Who

can bring a clean thing out of an unclean?' (14:4). If human initiative could produce the new birth, then a clean thing would come out of an unclean thing (see John 6:44 and 1 Cor. 2:14).

2. *Scripture everywhere attributes the new birth to God.* This is true in the Old Testament. God promises to give a new heart to Israel (Ezek. 36:26). The writing of the law on the heart, a part of the new covenant, is ascribed to the agency of God (Jer. 31:33). The psalmist says that God's people are willing or 'volunteers' in the day of God's power (Ps. 110:3).

The New Testament confirms positively that God makes dead sinners alive. Jesus compared salvation to a resurrection (John 5:25). Men are born 'of ... the Spirit' (John 3:5). The new birth is not of blood (natural relationship), nor of the will of the flesh (cannot be produced by a decision), nor of the will of man (someone else cannot save us), but of God (John 1:13). It is not of him that wills or of him who runs, but of God who shows mercy (Rom. 9:16). The Lord opened Lydia's heart so that she received the things taught by God's minister (Acts 16:14).

The mighty change of regeneration is a 'new creation' (2 Cor. 5:17) comparable to the first creation when the Holy Spirit 'was hovering over the face of the waters' (Gen. 1:2). The power that produced life in Christians is the same as that which was wrought in Christ and raised him from the dead (Eph. 1:20).

3. *Repentance and faith are gifts of God*

a. Repentance is given by God (Acts 5:31; 2 Tim. 2:25).
b. Faith is a gift of God. We are saved by grace through faith, which is the gift of God (Eph. 2:8-9). Believers have

obtained precious faith (2 Peter 1:1), through the operation of God (Col. 2:12).

The means of regeneration

Since the new birth is an inward and spiritual work bringing about a change in man's heart, the means or instrument must be such as can influence man's moral faculties (mind, will, etc.). It is *the truth,* applied by the Holy Spirit, which is the instrument of regeneration. The Word of God, or gospel, shows us our sin, tells us of God's requirements and reveals Christ.

It is the gospel message either written or spoken which enlightens men about their lost estate, convicts them of their sinfulness, and leads them to Christ, the sinner's substitute. It is of God's sovereign will that we are given new life through the gospel (1 Cor. 4:15). In the parable of the sower Jesus taught that the salvation of souls is like the sprouting and growing that results from the planting of seed. The seed represents the Word of God (Luke 8:11). Peter says that we are born again, not of corruptible seed, but of incorruptible, the Word of God that lives and abides for ever (1 Peter 1:23).

The nature of regeneration

1. *It is a spiritual change.* It is not the giving to man of a soul, he already has one. It is not the giving of faculties: mind, heart and will; he has these. It is not the addition of some new physical substance to the personality, or the soul of man. It is a work upon the inner being of man, producing a new direction to his moral nature.

2. *It is a total change.* When we say that man is totally depraved we do not mean that he is as bad as he can be, it means all parts of his being have been affected by sin. In the same

way, when we say that the new birth produces a total change we do not mean that man is as good as he can be when he is regenerated, we mean that all parts of his being are changed. His understanding is enlightened (2 Cor. 4:4; Eph. 1:18). The heart is turned from a state of self-love to love to God (1 John 4:19). The will is constrained from rebellion to submission (1 Thess. 1:9).

3. *It is an instantaneous change.* Regeneration is not a gradual work. Although the work of the Spirit that precedes it may be gradual, and may in fact go on for a long time, life comes in an instant. A person cannot be alive and dead at the same time; it is one or the other. Conviction is the ordinary antecedent to regeneration, but it does not necessarily lead to it. The sinner resists the Spirit till regenerated. The moment a soul is quickened it is born again (Eph. 2:1, 5).

4. *It is a change that is known by its results.* Obedience to Christ is the evidence of regeneration, as is overcoming the world, etc. (Heb. 5:9; 1 John 5:4).

Descriptions of regeneration

We can have a better understanding of the change wrought by the Spirit when we consider the various ways in which this change is described.

1. *A birth* (John 3:3). This shows that one who is regenerated has a new nature, enters into a new relationship, and in fact enters a whole new realm of living.

2. *Creation* (2 Cor. 5:17). The new birth is not an improvement upon the old nature, but a gift of something new, the implantation in man of a principle of life.

3. *Calling* (Rom. 8:28-30). This call is according to God's purpose. It is the middle link in the chain. The other links are foreknowledge, predestination, justification and glorification.

4. *Revelation* (Matt. 11:25; Matt. 16:17; 1 Cor. 2:9-10). To be able to see Christ with the eye of faith requires spiritual surgery by the Holy Spirit.

5. *Teaching* (John 6:45; 1 Cor. 2:13). The experience of being brought to salvation through Holy Spirit conviction and regeneration is a sort of school, in which God is the teacher and the believer is the learner.

6. *Sanctification* (1 Peter 1:2). This sanctification or 'setting apart' has an initial phase (when a person is first consecrated to God) and is a continual process.

7. *Resurrection* (John 5:25-26). When Jesus raised Lazarus from the dead, he pictured his power in raising sinners.

8. *Spiritual baptism* (1 Cor. 12:12-13). When the Holy Spirit comes upon a person and grants the new birth that person is submerged and enveloped in his power and made one with Christ and all other believers.

Union with Christ

The action of the Holy Spirit in bringing a person into a state of regeneration thereby establishes a connection between the believer and Christ, which can be described as a union. Over and over again the expression 'in Christ' appears in the New Testament. As A. H. Strong has said, this phrase 'in Christ', always meaning 'in union with Christ', is the very key to Paul's epistles, and the believer's relationship to the Lord. It is in Christ that we have spiritual life, a comprehensive term including the whole matter of deliverance from sin.

The book of Ephesians abounds with statements relating to the blessings we have through union with Christ. Paul says all our spiritual blessings 'in the heavenly places' are in Christ (Eph. 1:3). These include acceptance with God (1:6), redemption (1:7), forgiveness of sins (1:7), inheritance in Christ (1:11), sealing of the Holy Spirit (1:13), spiritual resurrection (1:19-20), reconciliation (2:16), access to the Father (2:18), and union with other Christians (2:21-22).

The fact of union with Christ

1. The believer is in Christ (John 14:20; Rom. 8:1; 2 Cor. 5:17).
2. Christ is in the believer (John 14:20; Rom. 8:10; Gal. 2:20).
3. The Father and the Son dwell in the believer (John 14:23).
4. The believer has life by partaking of Christ (John 6:53, 56).
5. All believers are one in Christ (John 17:21-23).

The nature of union with Christ

1. *It is an organic union.* We become partakers of Christ's life because he is alive and we live in him (organic means joined to a living organism).

2. *It is a vital union.* The bond of union between the believer and Christ is the gift of his Spirit to dwell in us (Rom. 8:9-10), and our faith in him (Eph. 3:17).

3. *It is a spiritual union.* It is a union not of bodies but of the mind, soul and spirit. The spirit of Christ in the believer causes him to think and act like Christ.

4. *It is an indissoluble union.* The union of the believer with Christ was not established by their works or agency, and neither can it be severed by any human agency. Christ will no more sever a part of his spiritual body than a human being in his right mind would cut off a part of his physical body (John 10:28; Rom. 8:35-39).

Pictures of union with Christ

The union of Christ and the believer is inscrutable and mysterious. It cannot be fully grasped by the human mind. But we can have a perception of it and there are pictures of this union in Scripture that clarify it.

1. *A building and its foundation.* Christ is represented in Scripture as a foundation with the church a spiritual house built upon him (Eph. 2:20-22; 1 Peter 2:4-5).

2. *Husband and wife.* The marriage bond is the closest earthly relationship. There is a bond between husband and wife that makes them legally and vitally one. This is a picture of the union of Christ and his people (Rom. 7:4; 2 Cor. 11:2; Eph. 5:31-32).

3. *A vine and its branches.* In John 15:5 Jesus said, 'I am the vine, you are the branches. He who abides in me, and I in him, bears much fruit; for without me you can do nothing.' Here is clearly a union of life force. The very life of the trunk flows through and invigorates each branch. The life

of Christ flows to and through us by the indwelling of the
Spirit and faith.

4. *Head and body* (1 Cor. 12:12). 'For as the body is one and
has many members, but all the members of that one body,
being many, are one body, so also is Christ.' 'Christ' here is
not Christ physical, but Christ mystical, the church (see also
Eph. 4:15-16; Eph. 5:30). As the head of the human body is
the dynamic source of all energy and sensation, so Jesus
Christ infuses life into the church, maintains its existence and
co-ordinates all its members.

6.
Learning about the Christian life

In this section we would like to concentrate on the truths of Scripture that relate to the believer's life and walk in this world. This is obviously a vast subject; a brief survey like this can only deal with the highlights. We will break the pertinent facts down into categories so that some of the main points can be seen. First of all, we will consider God's provision for the believer, and secondly, the believer's responsibility.

God's provision for the believer: security

Is one who has trusted Christ for salvation and become a child of God assured of final salvation? As we all know, this is a point on which Christian people have differed. Some claim that it is possible for a true child of God to lapse and become eternally doomed. We believe the opposite, that there is abundant biblical evidence that this cannot be the case.

Not all who profess salvation possess it

One thing that confuses some people is the fact that some who make a profession of faith, and give some evidence of

being regenerated, turn away from God and become wicked
people again. This we acknowledge to be a fact. But the question is: Were they truly saved in the first place? There are
cases like this in the Bible. For example, Judas, who lived in
the intimate company of Christ, eventually betrayed him. We
believe, however, that Judas was never a true believer. In John
6:70 Jesus anticipated Judas' apostasy and said, 'Did I not
choose you, the twelve, and one of you is a devil?'

Throughout Scripture we see that there is a possibility of
a superficial, temporary faith which does not save. According to James 2:19, even the devils believe, in some sense. In
John 8 we read that after Jesus had preached to some of his
countrymen, 'many believed in him' (v. 30). But notice the
response of the Lord to these 'believers': 'If you abide in my
word, you are my disciples indeed' (v. 31). Here Jesus makes
it clear that real disciples not only give mental assent to the
gospel, but obey as well.

The temporary believer is pictured very clearly in the parable of the sower (Matt. 13:1-23). In this parable, Jesus shows
the four possible effects of gospel preaching.

1. Sometimes the seed of the word falls by the wayside (v. 4).
   This is a picture of those on whom the word has no effect.

2. Sometimes the word falls into stony places where there is
   no depth of soil (v. 5). Although the seed sprouts quickly,
   it is soon scorched by the sun. Jesus explains this to mean
   that some, though initially receiving the word with joy,
   are discouraged by tribulation and persecution, and fall
   away (v. 21).

3. The third is similar, only the effect of the gospel is nulli-
   fied by 'the cares of this world and the deceitfulness of
   riches' (v. 22).

4. The fourth type is the true convert who understands the
   word and bears various degrees of fruit (v. 23).

Another thing we must keep in mind is the fact that people
may go far in religion and be unconverted. This is not the
place to deal with this subject at length, but in Hebrews and
such epistles as 2 Peter and Jude we can see that men may be
illuminated of the Holy Spirit (Heb. 6:4) and even possess
the 'knowledge of the Lord and Saviour, Jesus Christ', and
still fall away or desert their profession (see 2 Peter 2:20). A
true Christian, when reading these passages, might be inclined
to wonder whether he is truly saved. To some extent this is
good, for it is better to have honest doubts than to be sinfully
and presumptuously secure. Let us never forget that men may
know something about Christ, talk about him and give fine
testimonies, but not be truly born again.

Reasons for believing in the security of believers

1. The very nature of the blessing proves it is secure; it is
eternal life. The New Testament, particularly the Gospel of
John, asserts that the believer possesses a salvation that is
everlasting. Consider such verses as John 3:16; 3:36; and 5:24.
The last verse says, 'Most assuredly, I say to you, he who hears
my word, and believes in him who sent me has everlasting
life, and shall not come into judgement, but is passed from
death into life.' The word for life here is *zoe*; it has to do with
the *quality* of salvation, it is supreme *happiness.* The word
for 'everlasting' in the above texts is *ionios.* According to the
Liddell and Scott Greek-English Lexicon, this means, 'lasting, or eternal'. We could rest our case for eternal security
here and say nothing else. What a shame that such a blessed
truth as the security of the saints has become a subject of
controversy! Let us not argue but *rejoice.*

2. The power of the triune God is engaged in *preserving
believers*. The eternal salvation of God's people depends ultimately not on their own goodness but on the purpose, love,
grace and power of God. Jesus said in John 10:29 that his
Father is 'greater than all', and that no one could pluck his
sheep out of his Father's hand. Only if there is a power greater
than God can one of the sheep be separated from the Great
Shepherd.

a. *The purpose of the Father*. Ephesians 1:11 states that God
   works all things according to the 'counsel of his will'. The
   glorious truth of election means that all those who were
   given to Christ (John 6:37) will be secure in their salvation,
   because God has predetermined it. The saints of God are
   often tested, tempted and sometimes they even fall, but
   they will be 'kept' (1 Peter 1:5), 'preserved' (Jude 1), and
   'upheld' (Ps. 37:24). The whole of Psalm 37 abounds in
   promises of security to believers.

b. *The intercession of the Son*. Not only the Father but also
   the Son is engaged to keep believers. Both Judas and Peter
   were attacked by Satan before Christ's crucifixion. Both
   denied the Lord in one way or another. But Peter was forgiven, Judas was not. Why? Peter was a true believer, Judas
   was never converted, and though Satan desired to 'sift'
   Peter, Jesus prayed for him that his faith should not fail
   (Luke 22:32). 1 John 2:1 tells us that when a believer sins,
   he has an 'advocate' with the Father whose blood 'cleanses'
   from sin (1 John 1:7). Those for whom Jesus pleads cannot
   be lost. See his intercessory prayer in John 17, especially
   verse 9.

c. *The indwelling of the Spirit*. As soon as a person receives
   Christ as Saviour and Lord, the Holy Spirit comes in to

dwell (Acts 2:38). This is the beginning of a process that shall never end, for according to Philippians 1:6: 'He who has begun a good work in you will complete it until the day of Jesus Christ.' Though the Holy Spirit may be grieved (Eph. 4:30) and quenched (1 Thess. 5:19), he will never completely leave a Christian. Jesus said, 'And I will pray the Father, and he will give you another Helper, that he may abide with you for ever' (John 14:16). The believer is also sealed with the Holy Spirit. According to Ephesians 1:13, as soon as a person believes, he is 'sealed with the Holy Spirit of promise'. In the symbolism of Scripture a seal signifies: (1) a finished transaction (Jer. 32:9-10); (2) ownership (Jer. 32:11-12); and (3) security (Esth. 8:8; Dan. 6:17; Eph. 4:30). Clearly, one sealed by the Holy Spirit is destined for heaven, for the impress of divine ownership is upon him.

3. *A relationship is established* between God and his people *which cannot be dissolved.* Believers are referred to in the Bible as the children of God (Rom. 8:16). The word for child here is *teknon*, meaning one born. When a child is born of two people it will have the nature of those two parents for as long as it lives. Though legally it may belong to someone else, its *nature* cannot change. There is not the slightest indication in the Scriptures that one who is created in the image of Christ by the new birth (Col. 3:10) will ever lose that image. For this reason, the apostles rejoiced in the assurance of final salvation (see 1 John 3:2; Col. 3:4).

There is a difference in relationship and fellowship. The former depends on organic and legal connection, the latter on obedience. Through sin or backsliding, a believer can lose fellowship with God and also assurance. But provision can be made for sin and restored fellowship through the continuing ministry of Christ (1 John 1:7; 2:1).

4. There is no power in the universe that can sever *the connection between God and his people*. Jesus said that none could snatch his sheep from his Father's hand (John 10:29). In Romans 8:35-39 Paul raises the question of whether anything can separate a believer from Christ. Then he distinctly denies the possibility. He specifically lists a comprehensive group of potential enemies to the Christian: tribulation, distress, persecution, famine, nakedness, peril, sword, death, life, angels, principalities, powers, things present, things to come, height and depth. Can anyone imagine any phenomenon on heaven, earth, or hell that is not covered in this imposing list? Paul, as if in fear he might have left something out, adds in verse 39 'any other created thing'. Surely it takes daring audacity for any religious teacher to fly in the face of such an argument and claim that a believer in Christ may perish, after all.

God's provision for the believer: sanctification

There is a family of words in the New Testament which has the idea of holiness at the root. These words are the verb 'make holy' or 'sanctify', the adjective 'holy', a couple of words meaning sanctity, holiness, and one meaning sanctification. Holiness is clearly an essential part of being saved.

The three tenses of salvation

This is perhaps a good place to mention that 'salvation' is used in Scripture in three senses.

1. There is a sense in which we have already been saved, that is, from the *penalty* of sin. The past tense is used in such passages as 2 Timothy 1:9; and Ephesians 2:8 (this means,

'you have been saved and still are'). Through the redemption of Christ, believers are fully justified as an accomplished fact.

2. There is a sense in which we *are being saved*, referring to an ongoing process. Believers are now being saved from the habit and dominion of sin (Phil. 2:12-13; 1 Cor. 15:2 — 'you are being saved'; see Young's translation). The whole of Romans 6 deals with the ongoing process in which believers are being delivered from the power of sin in their lives. This is sanctification, the subject at hand.

3. There is a sense in which salvation is yet future; it is a goal, and that is the final phase of God's plan: salvation from the *presence* of sin. References to future salvation in Scripture can be found in 1 Corinthians 5:5; Romans 8:23; and 1 Peter 1:5. Twice in Romans (2:6-7; 6:22) Paul speaks of eternal life as the end or culmination of holy living. In heaven all sinfulness and infirmity will be removed from the bodies and souls of believers, thus they will be delivered from the presence of sin.

The meaning of sanctification

The first time the word 'sanctify' appears in our Bible is in Genesis 2:3 where we read that God blessed the seventh day and 'sanctified it'. The meaning here obviously is that God consecrated the seventh day or set it aside for a holy purpose. This shows us that *things* as well as *people* can be sanctified. This is, of course, a purely external act, since one day is inherently no more holy than any other day. Throughout the Old Testament we see certain physical objects being sanctified, such as the altar of the tabernacle (Exod. 29:36) and the tabernacle itself (Lev. 8:10).

But a moral element is obviously involved when the Bible talks about the sanctification of people. David called upon the Levites to 'sanctify' themselves (1 Chron. 15:12), and Jesus prayed in his priestly prayer that his people might be sanctified (John 17:19). 'Saints', or 'holy ones', is one of the titles of believers (Eph. 1:15), and 'the sanctified' is one of the names given to those who are in Christ (Acts 20:32). One of the programmes of Christ for his people is that he is sanctifying them, and making them ready for heaven (Eph. 5:26). Paul's prayer for the Thessalonians was that God would 'sanctify [them] completely' (1 Thess. 5:23). The central idea in all these words is that God is making people holy.

The two types of sanctification

The Scriptures speak of a positional or legal sanctification through the blood of Christ and a practical or experimental sanctification of the Holy Spirit through the Word. Let us look first at the positional aspect. Leviticus 8 explains the ceremony in which the priest was consecrated to his office. It took place when Aaron and his sons were sprinkled with oil and blood. This was a type or picture of the sanctification or setting apart of Christians through the blood of Christ. In the book of Hebrews, we are told that Jesus sanctified his people by the blood he shed on Calvary (Heb. 10:10; 13:12). Because the blood of Jesus Christ cleanses from sin when it is received by faith, it sanctifies or makes holy those who benefit from it. This shows us that *the blood of Christ* is the basis of sanctification. Note that the priests of the Old Testament were sanctified with oil and blood. The oil symbolizes the Holy Spirit. This means that the sacrifice of Christ and the Holy Spirit work in conjunction with each other; one is the basis of the other. Ironically, legal sanctification must precede practical sanctification.

Practical, experiential sanctification

Paul wrote to the Thessalonians that God had chosen to save them through sanctification of the Spirit and belief of the truth (2 Thess. 2:13). The elect of God are brought into a relationship with God by a sanctifying work of God's Holy Spirit. 1 Peter 1:2 tells us that believers are elect according to the foreknowledge of God the Father, through sanctification of the Spirit. Sanctification is the 'will of God' for the believer (1 Thess. 4:3).

1. *The nature of it.* Basically, sanctification is a continuation and development of the work of God in regeneration. The latter is the initial creation in the soul of man of a holy principle, consisting of love to God and its many outworkings. Sanctification is the outworking of that holy principle in the life and walk of the believer.

a. *It is both inward and outward.* God is concerned both about the believer's *heart* and *life*. Psalm 51 is one place where the importance of a consecrated heart is emphasized: 'Behold, you desire truth in the inward parts.' 'Create in me a clean heart, O God.' 'The sacrifices of God are a broken spirit; a broken and a contrite heart — these, O God, you will not despise' (vv. 6, 10, 17). Even in the midst of the giving of the law, God exhorted: 'Therefore circumcise the foreskin of your heart, and be stiff-necked no longer' (Deut. 10:16).

Although an inward conformity to God's will is an essential part of holiness, the will of God touches outward behaviour also. In Titus 2:10 the believers are exhorted to 'adorn the doctrine of God our Saviour, in all things'. This word 'adorn' means to decorate, garnish, or 'put in order', as seen in Matthew 12:44. It is also the same word that is

used in Titus 2:10. All of this has to do with external behaviour — such as the way we speak, dress and relate to
other people. In other words, sanctification has to do with
lifestyle.

b. *It is progressive, but not uniformly so.* Proverbs 4:18
shows this in an interesting way: 'But the path of the just
is like the shining sun, that shines ever brighter unto the
perfect day.' The life of a godly man is compared to the
course of the sun, starting, as it were, in the dim twilight
of morning and reaching out with ever-increasing brightness over the developing course of the day. Some of the
pictures we have of progressive sanctification are *growth*
(Mark 4:28; 2 Peter 3:18), *addition* (2 Peter 1:5), and
moving ahead along a path (Heb. 6:1). All of these figures of speech show progress, whether in the maturity of
a child to an adult, the addition of one element to another,
or forward movement on a road such as walking on a
pathway.

Progress involves knowledge. Scripturally speaking,
there is no such thing as progressive sanctification apart
from an increase of spiritual knowledge. Jesus said that
we are to come and 'learn of me' (Matt. 11:29). This education process is to continue throughout the Christian life.
In his exhortation of adding to our faith virtue, etc., Peter
stresses that such growth prevents one from being barren
and unfruitful 'in the knowledge of our Lord Jesus Christ'
(2 Peter 1:8). Also, the last exhortation of this epistle is
that we 'grow in the grace and knowledge of our Lord and
Saviour' (2 Peter 3:18).

c. *It is total.* All faculties are touched by sanctification. Earlier we pointed out that the will is reached through the
affections and the affections are reached through the mind.

The point is that the mind of man is the gate of his soul. As our minds are enlightened by the truth, the affections will be enlarged towards God, and the will shall be bent towards his commandments. In other words, progressive sanctification means *greater knowledge of the Lord,* as we study his Word and live in his presence; *greater love for him*, as we become more acquainted with his person; and *greater readiness* to choose that which is right as the Holy Spirit inclines our hearts to his service. Total sanctification does not mean absolute perfection any more than total depravity means that the sinner is as bad as he can be. Both wickedness and righteousness allow the possibility of degrees of attainment in this life.

d. *It leads to maturity.* The Bible unquestionably teaches the possibility of a Christian reaching a state of spiritual maturity in this life. The old word for maturity, as given in the Authorized Version, was 'perfect'. But the meaning of the word 'perfect' has changed. Rather than indicating something 'mature' or complete, now it has the connotation of something without flaw or without fault. When Paul said, 'We speak wisdom among them that are perfect' (1 Cor. 2:6, AV), he means one who is mature in thinking, as it is translated by the New King James Version. Paul's admonition to 'Be perfect, be of good comfort' (2 Cor. 13:11, AV) means 'Become complete. Be of good comfort' (NKJV). 'Let us go on unto perfection' (Heb. 6:1, AV), means 'Let us go on to maturity.' 'That the man of God may be perfect' (2 Tim. 3:17, AV) is translated by the NKJV 'that the man of God may be complete'. In these passages the reference is not to a final sinless state in heaven but something attainable in this life.

What is spiritual maturity? It is reaching an advanced or higher level in certain personal qualities. It means a higher level of faith. 'Praying exceedingly that we may see your face and perfect what is lacking in your faith' (1 Thess. 3:10). 'Perfect' or complete in Matthew 5:48 relates to loving others. 'That the man of God may be complete' in 2 Timothy 3:17 refers to being equipped for Christian service. 'Of full age' in Hebrews 5:14 speaks of discernment. According to James 3:2 the 'perfect' or mature person can bridle his tongue. According to James 1:4 the 'perfect' person, lacking in nothing, is patient. These passages show that growing to maturity involves increased faith, love, training in service, self-control and patience.

2. *The necessity of sanctification*

a. Sanctification is necessary for the same reasons that regeneration is necessary (see p. 105). Holiness is essential for fellowship with God, heaven would not be enjoyed without a new nature, and men cannot be happy without it.

b. The Bible teaches that holiness or sanctification is essential to salvation. There are many biblical statements to support this fact. Hebrews 12:14: 'Pursue peace with all people, and holiness, without which no one will see the Lord.' Ephesians 5:5 says that the unrighteous cannot inherit the kingdom of God. In John 14:21 Jesus said that all who love him keep his commandments. James 2:17 states that faith without works is dead, implying that works are necessary as an *evidence* of salvation. According to Romans 6:22 believers are 'free from sin', meaning not the *presence* of sin but the *power* of sin. We might add that in Ephesians 2:10 we are told that believers are created in Christ Jesus for good works, and that God has 'ordained' (AV), or 'prepared beforehand' (decreed, determined) that we carry them out.

What about 'carnal Christians'? In writing to the believers in Corinth Paul said, 'For you are still carnal' (1 Cor. 3:3). Some have concluded from this that 'carnal' is a separate category of Christians, as opposed to 'spiritual' ones. This view teaches that there are *three* kinds of people: *natural* or the unsaved; *spiritual* or obedient Christians; and *carnal* or disobedient Christians. In the light of the verses under point two this is an unscriptural notion. What Paul means in 1 Corinthians 3 is that the Christians in this particular circumstance were *acting in a carnal manner*. Even spiritual, or saved people, do this at times. In Romans 7:14 Paul himself claimed to be 'carnal'. What he meant was that he had a fleshly nature. The truth is that all Christians are both spiritual and carnal in one sense. They are spiritual in that God dwells in them, and they are in some measure obedient; but they are also 'carnal', in the sense that they have the flesh in them, and at times they yield to it.

3. *The means of sanctification.* How is sanctification brought about in a Christian's life? Three points seem to be pertinent.

a. *The Holy Spirit is the Author of it.* 2 Thessalonians 2:13 speaks of the sanctification of the Spirit.

b. *The Word of God is the means of it.* In his priestly prayer Jesus prayed, 'Sanctify them by your truth. Your word is truth' (John 17:17). Also, John 15:3: 'You are already clean because of the word which I have spoken to you.' Paul teaches in Ephesians 5:25-26 that Jesus Christ both loved and died for the church that he might 'sanctify and cleanse her with the washing of water by the word'.

c. In the New Testament the human side of sanctification is called *mortification*. To mortify means to put to death. In

Colossians 3:5 Christians are exhorted: 'Therefore put to death [mortify, AV] your members which are on the earth: fornication, uncleanness...' etc. The agency of the Christian is concerned here. He is called upon to stir up his mind, as it were, to the necessary but difficult task of suppressing the evil desires of his mind and flesh. Like sprouts and weeds in a garden, they may spring up again, but they must be cut down. This is in line with Christ's command to his disciples to 'deny' themselves, and take up the cross and follow him (Matt. 16:24). Perhaps the most graphic picture of the battle against sin is given by Jesus when he speaks of cutting off hands and plucking out eyes (Matt. 5:28-30). Here he teaches that one must chop off the sinful inclinations or suffer the pains of hell. In a day of easy and comfortable religion, this sounds harsh and strange.

God's provision for the believer: family discipline

There are, in society, what we might call 'community rules' and 'family rules'. They are always different. Because citizens are all under the same legal umbrella, they have a civic connection. They are bound by certain community rules. But there is a *special* relationship between members of the family. Rules within the household are in some instances stricter and yet this is because there is a greater *love-tie*. A parent will expect more from his child than from a neighbour's child, yet he also does more for his child.

So it is in the kingdom of God. God has placed all mankind under certain community rules, as it were. As Creator, God has the right to command respect from all men. Under strict principles of law, there are promises of reward for obedience and threats of condemnation for disobedience. Such is

God's relationship to men in general. Because man is a sinner, God has the relationship as both Creator and *Judge*. He is displeased with sinful humanity and warns the wicked of eternal judgement if they do not repent.

But believers are the *children of God*. Anyone who becomes a member of the family of God comes under a different set of rules because of this relationship. We call this set of rules 'family discipline'.

What is the meaning of *discipline*? Often when we hear the word 'discipline' we think of punishment. But this is a secondary meaning. The primary meaning is *training*. God's programme of training for his people means guidance and teaching, all in preparation for the ultimate goal: heaven. There are a number of important elements that go into God's disciplinary programme for his children, of which we shall now mention six that are essential.

The special ministry of the Holy Spirit

The work of the Holy Spirit before conversion is to convict the lost of sin and lead them to Christ. In regeneration, he gives a new nature and brings a person into union with Christ. After regeneration, the Spirit comes in to dwell within the believer. This is taught in many places, such as 1 Corinthians 3:16: 'Do you not know that you are the temple of God and that the Spirit of God dwells in you?' At the time of regeneration the indwelling Spirit begins a ministry in and for the Christian.

There is a special word used by Christ for the ministry of the Spirit in the Christian. Jesus said in John 14:26: 'But the Helper [AV, 'Comforter'], the Holy Spirit, whom the Father will send in my name, he will teach you all things, and bring to your remembrance all things that I said to you.' The word for 'comforter' here is *paraclete*. This Greek word means a

legal assistant in court, but it came to mean 'helper'. As our
'helper' the Holy Spirit of God graciously assists us in our
Christian pilgrimage.

1. *He teaches*. Jesus said that the Holy Spirit would teach
the disciples all things (John 14:26).
2. *He leads*. 'For as many as are led by the Spirit of God,
these are sons of God' (Rom. 8:14).
3. *He intercedes*. 'But the Spirit himself makes intercession
for us with groanings which cannot be uttered' (Rom. 8:26).
4. *He assures*. 'The Spirit himself bears witness with our
spirit that we are children of God' (Rom. 8:16).

The influence of the Word of God

Because the Bible is widely distributed and read, it has a re-
straining influence upon society. But it has a special purpose
in the life of the Christian. It is his food, special guidebook,
and light for living. It is by the Bible that God daily speaks to
his people.

There are certain parts of the Bible which are written to
bring men to God. (It is a primary purpose of the Gospel of
John; see 20:31.) But there are portions of the Bible that were
written to *believers*, and deal with how men should conduct
their lives after becoming Christians.

A happy, normal Christian life depends on Bible study.
Here are three types of Scripture material which are especially helpful in the training of the believer.

1. *The commands of the Bible*. In the Word, especially the
New Testament, the Christian finds out what is God's will.
An ignorant Christian is a weak Christian.
2. *The promises of the Bible*. Peter speaks of 'exceedingly
great and precious promises' (2 Peter 1:4). Reading the

promises of the Bible, storing them up in his mind, and believing them encourages the Christian and equips him to face life.

3. *The warnings of Scripture*. Often we do not appreciate a warning, but in all areas of life a warning may cause a person to avert danger. God's warnings keep his people cautious.

Prayer and communion

This is a very important factor in the training of believers. Prayer is the special privilege of those who are 'in Christ'. Through Christ, their 'elder brother', they have access into the presence of God. Through communion with their heavenly Father, believers receive strength for the battles of life and learn more of his gracious heart. At the throne of God's grace in prayer, there is comfort, solace and relief from the wounds of life. As the great hymn 'Sweet Hour of Prayer' says,

> In seasons of distress and grief,
>   my soul has often found relief,
> and oft escaped the tempter's snare,
>   by thy return, sweet hour of prayer.

The providence of God

Enlightened Christians are aware that there is a special guidance and protection working on their behalf. While 'The LORD is good to all, and his tender mercies are over all his works' (Ps. 145:9), he especially looks out for his children. He 'guides [them] with [his] eye' (Ps. 32:8). He shields them from the power of Satan. He cares for them. He clothes and feeds them (Matt. 6:28-34). He makes all things work together for their good (Rom. 8:28). When the believer learns to appreciate God's providential care, and accepts it by faith, he has learned an important lesson in God's training.

The church of God

God's people are not dogs, which often run about alone, but a *flock of sheep*. They find strength and instruction by association with other Christians. In the church they hear the Word of God proclaimed, pray with others and join in singing songs of praise to their God. A Christian outside the church (if there is such a thing) is an abnormal, unhappy, stunted person. The church is the training ground for service.

Afflictions

Such is the situation here on earth that God must send trials into the lives of believers to train them. This does not necessarily mean that all afflictions are disciplinary. Actually there are three reasons for the trials God sends.

1. *They prove.* As gold is tried and purified in the fire, so difficulties test and bring out the best in Christians (1 Peter 1:7).
2. *They prevent.* Often we are kept out of trouble by the gracious hand of the Lord in sending trouble (Ps. 119:67).
3. *They chasten.* It is an evidence of God's love when he chastens his people after they stray. 'Whom the LORD loves he chastens' etc. (Heb. 12:6).

The believer's responsibility

God has graciously provided for the welfare of his children in this world. But they are also responsible to their Redeemer and Lord. Here are some critical areas of responsibility for the believer.

With reference to perseverance in holiness

Although the salvation of the believer is final in the absolute sovereign purpose of God, and although justification is a final, irrevocable fact, there is a sense in which salvation is yet future. When Paul says that 'our salvation is nearer than when we first believed' (Rom. 13:11), he clearly is not talking about justification but the final deliverance from sin in heaven. Salvation is used also in a future tense (Heb. 1:14; 1 Peter 1:5, 9).

1. Salvation in the future sense of complete deliverance from sin is conditioned upon holiness, or continuing in grace. Obedience to the Lord, or good works, are the evidence of the sovereign work of God in the heart. The life of obedience and faith leads to heaven. A godly life does not merit the grace of God in any way, but it puts a believer in the way of eternal life or salvation in the ultimate sense. Romans 6:22 says, 'But now having been set free from sin, and having become slaves of God, you have your fruit to holiness, and the end, everlasting life.' 'Everlasting life' here is not justification; that is final when a person is converted. It is the final state in heaven.

2. Proof of the necessity of perseverance in grace for final salvation.

a. *Conversion* involves turning from and hating sin. Peter called on the sorcerer Simon to repent of his wickedness as a condition of his being forgiven (Acts 8:22). Paul gives 'turning to God from idols' as a sign and evidence that the Thessalonians had been truly converted (1 Thess. 1:9).

b. *Saving grace* is a prevailing principle. When a person is converted he is 'overcome' by Christ, and Satan's power is dispossessed (Luke 11:21-22). Christ, who dwells in the believer, is greater than the devil (1 John 4:4).

c. *Good works* are an essential evidence of salvation. Jesus said that only those who do the will of God will enter the kingdom of heaven (Matt. 7:21). The second chapter of James is devoted to teaching that a faith that does not produce good works is dead (see vv. 20, 24).

d. *Continuance in the faith* shows the genuineness of faith. Paul tells the Colossians that their profession is credible if they 'continue in the faith' (Col. 1:23). Who are those who belong to the spiritual 'house' of Jesus? According to Hebrews 3:6, those who 'hold fast the confidence and the rejoicing of the hope firm to the end'.

e. *Continuing in sin is inconsistent* with a state of grace. The Christian is not only 'dead to sin' — that is, legally delivered from guilt through Christ's atonement (Rom. 6:11), but also 'free from sin', that is, free from the dominating influence of sin in his life (6:18). Those who are born of God do not practise sin as a way of life (1 John 3:9). Falling into sin, or committing a transgression, is not the same as practising or continuing in sin.

f. *Eternal reward* is promised to those who overcome. Galatians 6:8 states that those who sow to the flesh reap corruption, but those who sow to the Spirit reap everlasting life. This is salvation in the future sense. In Revelation, to each of the seven churches of Asia the promise of eternal blessings in heaven, under various symbols, is offered to those who overcome (2:7; 2:11; 2:17; 2:26; 3:5; 3:12; 3:21).

With reference to a relationship with God

1. *The Christian and the law.* The believer is still under the moral law as a rule of life. 1 John 3:4 tells us that sin is lawlessness. Since the believer has to confess sin, then the law is still in force (1 John 1:9). The believer delights in the law of God and strives to keep it (Rom. 7:22), but falls far short of its perfect demands (Rom. 7:24-25).

2. *The Christian and prayer.* Prayer is both a duty and a privilege. Immediately upon his conversion, Paul began to pray (Acts 9:11). Jesus took it for granted that his disciples would pray (Matt. 6:5).

3. *The Christian and self-denial.* Crucifying the flesh with its affections and lusts is the mark of a believer (Gal. 5:24). Jesus made self-denial a condition of discipleship (Matt. 16:24).

4. *The Christian and worship.* Jesus told the woman at the well that God is seeking worshippers (John 4:23). Both the Old Testament saints and the New Testament believers were worshippers of God. 'We are the circumcision, who worship God in the Spirit,' said Paul (Phil. 3:3).

With reference to a relationship with men

1. *Other members of the human race.* The essence of God's will is summed up in love: love to God and love to neighbours (Matt. 22:37-39). No outward works are of any value without this love (see 1 Cor. 13). All men (1 Thess. 3:12), even enemies (Matt. 5:44), are to be loved with good will and benevolence.

2. *Civil government.* Jesus Christ never established any particular type of civil or social order. He did, however, teach his disciples to pay taxes (Matt. 22:21). Paul admonishes Christians to submit to governing authorities (Rom. 13:1), as does Peter (1 Peter 2:13-17). When civil authorities infringed on their worship privileges, however, the early Christians had no qualms about disobeying them (Acts 4:20; 5:29).

3. *Christian brethren.* Jesus admonished his disciples to love each other (John 13:34) and made this the primary way the world could know who his disciples really were (John 13:35; see also 1 Peter 2:17). Loving other believers is a ground of assurance (1 John 3:14).

4. *Members of the family.* Responsibilities of husbands, wives and children are outlined by Paul in Ephesians 5:22-33 and 6:1-4. The primary responsibility of husbands is to be loving (5:25). Wives are commanded to be submissive (5:22). Children are to obey parents (6:1). See also Colossians 3:18-25.

5. *Employment relationships.* Masters (roughly equivalent to employers) are to pay just wages (Col. 4:1). Servants (applicable to employees) are to obey their masters in all things, as unto the Lord (Col. 3:22). John the Baptist told soldiers to be content with their wages (Luke 3:14).

With reference to the dimensions of their own personality

Self-love is recognized in the Bible as fundamental to human nature (Matt. 22:39) and is taken for granted. A man or woman of God is responsible for their own care in all dimensions of life: physical, psychological and spiritual. Jesus set the standard by growing in wisdom, stature and in favour with God and man (Luke 2:52). The spiritual aspect, loving and serving God, is paramount (Deut 6:5; Deut 6:13). The psychological dimension is addressed by all the passages that admonish the believer to trust in the Lord and not worry (Isa. 26:3; Matt. 6:25-34). A careful study of Philippians 4 will provide any Christian with a sound basis for relief from anxiety. Since the body is made by God and is indwelt by the Holy Spirit (1 Cor. 6:19) it should be looked after. Bodily exercise is profitable (1 Tim. 4:8). Eating and drinking to excess are condemned (Prov. 23:2, 29-33).

With reference to time

Time is a gift of God. We are to 'redeem' it, that is, purchase it like buying a commodity in the marketplace, and using it to the best advantage (Eph. 5:16). A pattern of daily devotion and worship is set for believers by the conduct of the saints of Scripture. David said, 'Evening and morning and at noon I will pray, and cry aloud, and he shall hear my voice' (Ps. 55:17). Under the Mosaic dispensation there were many special days for the Israelites to keep. Under the New Covenant, legalistic day-keeping is rebuked (Gal. 4:10; Col. 2:16-17), but liberty to use days for Christian worship and service is allowed (Rom. 14:5-6). It was the custom of the early church to meet for worship on the first day of the week (Acts 20:7) and to take up collections for the poor (1 Cor. 16:2). At the end of the first century the first day of the week had become known as the Lord's Day (Rev. 1:10).

With reference to stewardship

The Old Testament believers were commanded to give a tenth of their increase to the Lord (Lev. 27:30), and were to honour the Lord with the 'firstfruits' of their increase (Prov. 3:9).

Jesus taught his disciples that it is better to give than to receive (Acts 20:35). In 2 Corinthians 8 and 9 Paul gives extensive instructions to the early church on how they were to express generosity. Giving should be regular and proportionate to prosperity (1 Cor. 16:2), lavish (2 Cor. 9:6) and cheerful (2 Cor. 9:7).

With reference to evangelism

Jesus commanded the apostles to go into all the world and preach the gospel to all men (Matt. 28:16-20; Mark 16:15-16; Luke 24:46-49; Acts 1:8). This responsibility is both individual, that is, for the Christian as a private person, and for the church corporately. It is evident that the duty to share the gospel with all men was not limited to the apostles for Jesus promised to be with his people in the task of gospel preaching and missions 'even to the end of the age' (Matt. 28:20). The book of Acts chronicles how the early church, through Peter, John and others, but especially Paul, went everywhere preaching the word (Acts 5:42). Paul, who was so dramatically saved en route to persecute the church, as recorded in Acts 8, models for all believers in a remarkable way the passion they should have to save souls. His heart's desire for his people the Jews was that they might be saved (Rom. 10:1). He felt a debt to God and the world to 'preach the gospel' (Rom. 1:14-15). He testified that he was willing to become a servant to all that he might win them to Christ (1 Cor. 9:19-23). Such an example should be followed by all Christians.

7.
Learning about the church

Looking through the New Testament we can see that the church has a prominent place in the purpose of God for this age. 'Church' appears about 115 times in the New Testament. Jesus' promise to build his church indicates the importance he put upon this institution. He said, 'And I also say to you that you are Peter, and on this rock I will build my church, and the gates of Hades shall not prevail against it' (Matt. 16:18).

The necessity of the church

The nature of man

The church of Christ is necessary because of the nature of man. When God made the first solitary man, he looked at him and said that it was not good for man to dwell *alone*. His nature cried out for fellowship and companionship. This was fulfilled in the domestic relationship. But the human social instinct reveals itself when one becomes a person of faith. Believers naturally seek out others who share a common faith.

The nature of worship

The church of God is necessary because of the nature of worship. *Private* religion is important, but a sincere person will also go *public* with his convictions. Faith in God will necessarily find expression in *corporate* worship.

1. The earliest form of corporate, or collective, worship was in the family. In the patriarchal period Abraham, Isaac and Jacob led their families in sacrificial offerings and service to God. Of Abraham it is said, 'For I have known him, in order that he may command his children and his household after him, that they keep the way of the LORD, to do righteousness and justice, that the LORD may bring to Abraham what he has spoken to him' (Gen. 18:19). After his return from Haran, Jacob found his family in a backslidden state, and he 'housecleaned', as it were, setting his home in order spiritually (see Gen. 35:2).

2. In the days of the theocratic kingdom of Israel, the people worshipped God as a nation, and the tabernacle and temple were the centres of divine worship. This system was still in effect in the days of Jesus.

3. Now the local church is the focal point of divine worship. When the apostles went into the world and won men to Christ they always established *churches*. The new Christians were not left to wander about like stray sheep.

The nature of this age

The church is necessary because of the nature of this age. As long as the true religion was confined to one nation (Israel), a tabernacle or temple, with localized worship in Palestine, was sufficient. But God knew that the world's population would some day increase tremendously and this mode of worship would be inadequate and inconvenient. The Old Testament had promised that the Messiah would bless all nations. For this to come about, a new institution had to be founded.

1. The apostles preached that Jesus would usher in a new age and in the process do away with the Old Testament legal system. Jesus fulfilled the Old Testament sacrifices (called a 'shadow', Heb. 8:5) and 'changed the law' (Heb. 7:12), becoming the great priest after the order of Melchizedek (Heb. 7:11). Jesus 'wiped out' the Old Testament legal system (Col. 2:14) and tore down the wall of partition separating Jew and Gentile (Eph. 2:14).

2. In Ephesians 2 Paul shows us that the genius of the church is that it can adapt to any culture, language or nation, and thus was designed of God to be a *worldwide organism*. Jesus commissioned his disciples to take the gospel to all nations, and the church is adapted to receive people on the basis of faith alone, not any cultural or ethnic peculiarity.

The nature of the church

The meaning of ekklesia

The word for church in the New Testament is *ekklesia*. It is translated 'church' 112 times and 'assembly' three times (in the Authorized Version). The original usage of this word goes back to the Greek city states such as Athens and Sparta. They

were democratic in government, and when there was to be
official community business a man called the 'town crier' went
through the streets 'calling out' the people to the meetings.
This explains the word *ekklesia*: '*ek*' means out, and '*klesia*'
means calling. The church is thus a called-out body. The word
ekklesia came to mean assembly, referring to an assembly of
people 'called out' to transact official business. It is this word
which Jesus and the apostles used to describe the church.

The universal assembly

Several times in the New Testament, particularly in the book
of Ephesians, the writers conceived of all Christians as a kind
of ideal assembly. For example, Ephesians 5:25 says that
'Christ also loved the church and gave himself for her.' The
goal of God's redemptive purpose for the church is 'that he
might present her to himself a glorious church, not having
spot or wrinkle or any such thing, but that she should be holy
and without blemish' (Eph. 5:27). The Lord is not going to
present local churches, as such, to himself at his return, but
he will present all the redeemed as his bride. All God's
people, all those chosen by Christ and justified in his name,
will make up the great universal church. They are 'called out'
(see Acts 15:14; Rom. 8:28) to be the special possession of
the Lord.

The local assembly

Over and over again we see in the New Testament that
ekklesia, the church, is used in a literal sense to describe an
assembly of Christians. Many of the letters of Paul were written to such assemblies. Revelation chapters 2 and 3 were
addressed to the local 'churches' in Asia.

1. Christian people have, through the ages, organized and launched many organizations to carry out the work of the Lord. There are mission societies, seminaries, colleges, laymen's groups, youth ministries, children's ministries, book ministries, etc. These thing are good, no doubt the Lord has led in their establishment. But it is interesting to note that *Christ himself* founded only one organism, that is, the *local church*. All the work spoken of in the book of Acts and the epistles were carried out by *churches*.

2. A careful study of the New Testament shows that, just like churches today, no two of them were alike. Some were large (such as the church at Jerusalem, the mother church), and some were small (such as the one which met in the house of Nymphas, Col. 4:15). Some were in unity (see 1 Thess. 1) and some were sadly divided (see 1 Cor. 3:3). Some were thriving (such as the church at Philadelphia, Rev. 3:7-13) and some were nearly dead (such as the church at Sardis, Rev. 3:1-6). Some were orthodox in doctrine, others torn with heresy. Some were strict, some were lenient. Some were generous, others apparently not generous.

3. In spite of their differences, the churches of the New Testament period had some similarities. They all held to the doctrine of Christ (2 John 10), they all professed faith in Jesus Christ (as far as the record goes) by following the Lord in baptism, and they were all separate, distinct and autonomous. The authority of the apostles was a sort of unifying force, but the later development of church hierarchies, or associations, was unknown.

There is no evidence that there existed in New Testament days a supra-church structure such as a synod, conference or presbytery.

The constituents of the church

The New Testament our pattern

1. In the book of Exodus we are told that Moses went up onto Mount Sinai where he stayed forty days and nights. While there God delivered to him, in great detail, the laws that were to govern his people Israel. This included the *pattern for the construction of the tabernacle* (Exod. 25:9). After God finished giving these plans, Moses was charged as follows: 'And see to it that you make them according to the pattern which was shown you on the mountain' (25:40).

We learn from the New Testament that this was all a shadow or example of heavenly things, which are fulfilled in Christ (Heb. 8:5).

2. In a somewhat similar fashion, the New Testament spells out the *pattern for the congregations* founded by the apostles. We are not to go back to the law of Moses to find out how the church is to be operated, but to the New Testament, particularly the book of Acts, and the epistles.

No detailed instructions

You will notice that there are no *detailed* instructions about Christian church activity as there were concerning the legal worship of the Old Testament. For example, there are no New Testament rules about diet as in the Old Testament. Nor are there any specific details about day-keeping, buildings for worship, how often to take communion, order of worship, specific dress regulations, and methods in evangelism or education, such as Sunday schools or theological seminaries.

The point is, that in the New Testament there is a much larger area of Christian liberty. Great doctrinal themes are supplied, and basic guidelines are given, but not minute instructions on lifestyle and conduct. God ordained that the church be led by the Holy Spirit in harmony with the spirit of the gospel.

This is not to say the Christian has no rules or laws to live by. But under the new covenant of Christ the church is directed in a different way from the legalistic system that governed the people under the Mosaic economy. The responsibilities of believers in all their relationships — private, domestic and corporate — can be known in two ways.

1. *By specific command.* In such matters as church attendance (Heb. 10:25), baptism (Matt. 28:19), observing the Lord's Supper (1 Cor. 11:23-26), and submission to legitimate authority (Rom. 13:1), the apostles make clear the will of Jesus, the Lord of the church.

2. *By apostolic example.* What Christ and the apostles *did*, as well as what they taught, established a pattern of activity and Christian conduct. The early church met for worship on the first day of the week (Acts 20:7), sent out missionaries (Acts 13:2), and received collections for the poor (2 Cor. 8). Clearly this was intended to be an example for churches throughout this age.

What does the New Testament teach about the constituency of the church?

1. *It consists of those who have professed faith in Jesus Christ.* The teachings of Jesus, the history of the church in the book of Acts and the teachings of the apostles in their various epistles lead us to believe that God intended the church to consist exclusively of believers. Infants and people near the church who were merely sympathetic but not overly

committed to the gospel were not, in ideal at least, to be admitted to the church. We can see this from the following facts.

a. *Faith precedes baptism.* Notice the order in the great commission. The order of the gospel as set forth by Jesus Christ is that, first, people were to become disciples (through conversion) and then they were to be baptized (Matt. 28:19). Philip required belief before he baptized the eunuch (Acts 8:36-37). The Philippian jailer and his house believed, before they were baptized (Acts 16:31-33). From these examples we see that both in theory and practice only those who had accepted Christ as Saviour and Lord were baptized.

b. Acts 2:47 says the 'saved' were added to the church.

c. The church is a *covenanted* body. The church is to 'receive' people into their fellowship (Rom. 14:1). This shows us that any assemblage or group of Christians is not necessarily a church. To be truly a church a group of Christians must have agreed together to serve the Lord together in a special, covenanted *relationship.* But only believers should enter into such a covenant.

2. *They were baptized in the name of the Father, Son and Holy Ghost.* While the New Testament nowhere specifically states that the person should be baptized before being received into the church, the pattern and example of church activity sets this forth (Acts 2:41; 8:12-13; 9:18; 10:48, etc.).

Officers in the church

The various positions and gifts of those who make up the body of Christ are listed in such places as 1 Corinthians 12:7-

11; Ephesians 4:7-13; 1 Timothy 3; and Titus 1. These gifts are *diverse* and are distributed according to the sovereign good pleasure of God (1 Cor. 12:4, 11). *All* Christians have gifts (see Rom. 12:3-8), but some gifts involve *positions* in the church. Some who have gifts do not have leadership positions. All are important, however, and all contribute to the health and growth of the body of Christ (1 Cor. 12:12-31).

The temporary offices

The incarnation of Jesus Christ, his earthly life, death and resurrection, and his establishment of the church in the world created special and unusual circumstances. It was fitting that such an important and dramatic procedure as the inauguration of the Christian movement be accompanied by unusual power. God designed that the church should have an auspicious launching, and he put his stamp of approval upon it by giving it special gifts. The uniqueness of the apostolic office illustrates this fact.

1. *Apostles were unique.* They filled a special place in the history of the kingdom of God. After this purpose was fulfilled the office passed away. There was no need for them before this, and there has been no need since.

a. *They had a unique calling.* They were chosen directly and personally by Jesus Christ (Mark 3:13-14; Acts 9:6, 15; Rom. 1:1). God's method of selecting apostles is illustrated in the commissioning of Paul and Barnabas. The Holy Spirit instructed the church directly to set them apart for service (Acts 13:3).

b. *They had a unique experience.* The New Testament implies that the apostles had seen the Lord Jesus personally and had been witnesses of his resurrection (see Acts 1:22). Paul affirmed that he had seen Jesus Christ, thus establishing his claim to the apostolic office (1 Cor. 9:1).

c. *They had unique credentials.* 2 Corinthians 12:12 says, 'Truly the signs of an apostle were accomplished among you with all perseverance, in signs and wonders and mighty deeds.' When Jesus sent the twelve apostles out he gave them the power to heal the sick, raise the dead, cast out demons, etc. (Matt. 10:1, 8). These miraculous gifts served to *confirm* to the world the authenticity of the apostolic gospel (Heb. 2:3-4).

d. *They had unique authority.* Jesus gave the apostles powers of binding and loosing in the kingdom of God (Matt. 18:18; John 20:21-23). This implied infallible guidance in certain spiritual matters in the New Testament church. Paul charges the Corinthians to obey his instructions, since they are the commandments of the Lord (1 Cor. 14:37). John spoke *as an apostle* when he said, 'We are of God, he who knows God hears us; he who is not of God does not hear us' (1 John 4:6). They also had the power to convey spiritual gifts by the laying on of hands (Acts 8:18).

The higher endowments of the Spirit, the peculiar authority and the special guidance they claimed, set the apostles apart as temporary officers in the church. High church groups, such as the Roman Catholics, have claimed apostolic succession. They have also always claimed to have miraculous phenomena in the church (appearances of Mary, real blood coming from statues, etc.). Historically, attempts to revive the extraordinary gifts have ended up in confusion and fanaticism. With the completion of the canon of Scripture, the apostolic office and its attendant gifts passed away.

2. *The prophetic office was unique*

a. Whereas the apostolic office is restricted to the New Testament, the prophetic office was exercised both in the Old and New. Enoch the seventh from Adam was a prophet (Jude 14), and so was Moses (Hosea 12:13).

b. What was a prophet? Basically a prophet was one who went forth to deliver God's message to men. Both in the Old and New Testament there were women who prophesied; they were known as *prophetesses* (e.g. Miriam, Exod. 15:20; the daughters of Philip the evangelist, Acts 21:9). The primary function of the prophetic office was not so much *fore*telling, as *'forth*telling'; that is, the prophet appeared on the scene to 'give forth' or share God's message for his community and generation. Visions of the future were a part of his endowment, although not always.

c. In the process of God's progressive revelation — that is, the delivery of his word to mankind — prophets received a special inspiration and guidance. This special divine influence is referred to in 2 Peter 1:21. There were numerous ways this was expressed. Ezekiel 11:5 explains how this prophet was commissioned. 'Then the Spirit of the LORD fell upon me, and said to me, "Speak! 'Thus says the LORD...'"' etc. At such times the thoughts and visions of the prophet went beyond his own powers of knowledge. Another expression, especially used by Jeremiah, is 'the word of the LORD came to me' (Jer. 2:1). God's prophetic message often came also in the way of a dream or vision, as in the case of Daniel (Dan. 7:1). *Normally*, this inspiration was received by good men, but sometimes even by evil men, as in the case of Balaam (Num. 24:2).

With the completion of God's special revelation, the Bible, this form of revelatory prophecy ended. Daniel prophesied (9:24) that the vision and prophecy would be 'sealed up'.

d. The special inspiration known as prophecy continued in the New Testament church. Agabus was told by the Holy Spirit that Paul would be bound when he went to Jerusalem (Acts 21:11). Certainly the apostle John's visions in Revelation were prophetic. But if we remember that the primary meaning of prophet is 'forthteller', one delivering God's message, we may say that any preacher who gives public instruction in the Word of God is prophesying. It is clear from 1 Corinthians 14 that one who was prophesying was simply edifying the church (v. 4). This contrasts with the power to speak in foreign languages, which was a 'sign' to the unbeliever (1 Cor. 14:22).

The permanent offices in the church

Whereas the apostles and inspired public prophets were necessary for the church during the time God's revelation was being made known, some offices were for the church in a permanent and settled state, and therefore also for a church with a *completed Bible*.

1. *Pastor/bishop/elder/teacher*. The word for pastor means 'shepherd'. This word stresses the work of the minister: he cares for the Lord's people who are like sheep. The word for bishop means overseer. It stresses the authority of one in this position. The word elder means, as the word indicates, one advanced in age. This emphasizes the dignity of the office.

a. These are identical in nature. In 1 Peter 5:1-5 Peter addresses his exhortations to the 'elders' which were among the Christians to whom he is writing. In verse 2 he says, 'shepherd the flock of God', which means literally to 'pastor' or 'feed' the flock. In the same verse he says 'serving as overseers'. This literally means 'be bishops' within the church. Thus we see that pastor, elder and bishop mean the same thing.

In Acts 20 the three terms are similarly identified. Before Paul went to Jerusalem he 'called for the elders of the church' (20:17). Notice the exhortation to them in verse 28: 'Therefore take heed to yourselves and to all the flock, among which the Holy Spirit has made you overseers, to shepherd the church of God which he purchased with his own blood' etc. Overseers means bishops, and the word for 'feed' is, as just explained, pastor or shepherd.

b. There was a plurality of elders in each church. Contrary to the practice of most Baptist churches today, in the apostolic church each church had several elders. There is no case in which a church had only one elder. For Scripture proof see Acts 11:30; 14:23; 15:4; 16:4; 20:17; and Titus 1:5. Notice Acts 14:23: 'So when they had appointed elders in every church,' etc. There is evidence, however, that among the elders in each church one had a leadership position among equals. James was the spokesman for the men at Jerusalem (Acts 15:13). Each church in the book of Revelation had an 'angel' or messengers, which evidently refers to the primary leaders (e.g. Rev. 2:1). As we shall see by the next point it is difficult for all the responsibilities of the office of the elder to fall on one man.

c. *The functions of pastor/bishop/elder*

   • They are to rule in God's house (1 Tim. 3:4-5; 5:17). The authority, however, is not personal but in God's Word.

- They are to teach, as we see from Ephesians 4:11. In this passage 'pastor and teacher' seems to be equivalent to 'pastor/teacher'. One of the qualifications of a bishop is that he must be able to teach (1 Tim. 3:2). The elders are to feed or shepherd the flock of the Lord, not as lords or dictators but as examples (1 Peter 5:2-3).
- They are to be esteemed highly (1 Thess. 5:13), honoured (1 Tim. 5:17) and obeyed (Heb. 13:17).

2. *Deacons*

a. 1 Timothy 3:8-13 mentions the office and qualifications for deacons. Philippians 1:1 refers to the 'bishops and deacons' who were at Philippi. The central idea in the word deacon is service. The Greek word *diakonos* is sometimes translated servant, sometimes minister, and sometimes deacon.

b. The origin and function of this office are described in Acts 6:1-6. As can be seen, a problem arose concerning the care of widows in the church. The apostles felt that others than themselves should attend to this matter. 'It is not desirable that we should leave the word of God, and serve tables' (v. 2). Here we see a development of a twofold concern of the church: spiritual matters, and secular matters. The apostles, who served as ministers, felt that they should attend to 'prayer and to the ministry of the word' (v. 4). Seven men were chosen to take care of the business of 'serving tables' (v. 2). This is the work of the deacons. They are to handle the business and material matters of the church so that the elders can give themselves to preparation for the teaching of the Word.

3. There are many opportunities for *service by women* in the church. They can privately minister (Luke 8:3), teach (Acts 18:26; Titus 2:3), and do works of charity (Acts 9:36). The daughters of Philip prophesied (Acts 21:9). Phoebe was a 'servant' of the church at Cenchrea (Rom. 16:1). The word for servant here is the female form of deacon, which points to a position of deaconess in the church. Women are usually the greatest prayer warriors in the church. They joined in the prayer meetings with the brethren who were meeting in the upper room (Acts 1:14). Although there are restrictions on women relating to public preaching offices (1 Tim. 2:11-15; 1 Cor. 14:34-35), there is nothing in the Scriptures to forbid them from praying and testifying in the meetings of the church.

4. *Evangelists*. There is another office mentioned in the New Testament which may well constitute a third permanent office in the church. Evangelist is mentioned in Acts 21:8; Ephesians 4:11; and 2 Timothy 4:5. The word itself means simply a preacher of the gospel. The commonly received view is that evangelists were itinerant preachers, that is, preachers who went from place to place rather than settling in one church like a pastor. Charles Hodge says, 'They were properly missionaries sent to preach the Gospel where it had not been previously known.'[10]

Ordinances in the church

We are using the term ordinance in the sense of 'a symbolic rite or observance in the church'. The word is not used in this sense in Scripture, however, except perhaps in 1 Corinthians 11:2 (AV). The word here is translated 'traditions' in later versions. Throughout Protestantism it is recognized that Jesus left two ordinances in the church: baptism and the Lord's Supper. There are some evangelical Christians who hold that the public washing of feet is a church ordinance, based on John 13:14. Yet in New Testament days the washing of feet was a social custom based on the fact that people walked on dusty roads and wore only sandals. When they arrived from a journey to a home or public place their feet would be dirty. Jesus is teaching *service* on a private basis in John 13, not establishing an ordinance in the church.

Baptism

This ordinance is peculiar to the New Testament since no mention is made of it in the Old Testament. It was first administered by John the Baptist, who said, 'I indeed baptize you with water' (Matt. 3:11). According to Matthew 3:6 many from the region of the Jordan valley came to him 'confessing their sins'. They were also baptized 'unto repentance' (v. 11). 'Unto' (*eis*) here can be translated at or 'because of' (see Matt. 12:41 where the people of Nineveh repented 'at' [*eis*] the preaching of Jonah). In other words, John demanded that those who submitted to his baptism give evidence of repentance and a change of living (Matt. 3:8).

When Jesus sent out his disciples in what has been called the 'great commission', he charged them to do three things:

1. *Make disciples,* that is, lead them to a saving knowledge of the Lord (Matt. 28:19);
2. *Baptize,* in the name of the Father, Son and Holy Ghost (v. 19);
3. *Teach* the disciples after they are converted to obey the commands of Jesus (v. 20).

In Mark 16:16 Jesus said, 'He who believes and is baptized will be saved; but he who does not believe will be condemned.' This shows that baptism is obligatory for believers.

1. *The proper subjects of baptism.* There is one and only one qualification for baptism, and that is a conversion experience, or faith. This is seen:

a. *By the order of the great commission.* Jesus said first to make disciples and then to baptize them;
b. *By the baptism examples of the New Testament.* The apostles and disciples of Christ were, in the book of Acts, carrying out Jesus' command.

In every case of baptism, conversion preceded it (Acts 2:41; 8:12-13; 9:18; 16:14-15, 31-33). There is no biblical warrant for the baptism of infants.

2. *The proper mode of baptism.* Baptism as practised by the first Christians was immersion in water.

a. This is seen *by the meaning of the Greek word* baptizo, translated 'baptize' in the New Testament. The *Liddell and Scott Greek-English Lexicon* gives only one meaning of baptize: 'to dip'.

b. *By the symbolism of baptism.* Baptism is a picture of the gospel, which is summed up in 1 Corinthians 15:3-4: Christ died for our sins, was buried and rose again. The only way this can be pictured is for a person to be buried, or dipped. Romans 6:4 states that we are 'buried with him through baptism into death', and in Colossians 2:12 we find the expression 'buried with him in baptism'. Both passages also speak of being risen with Christ.

c. Baptism is immersion as seen *by the circumstantial evidence* in which the instances of actual baptism took place. If baptism is by pouring or sprinkling, the administrator would only need a bottle of water. But baptism as actually performed in the Bible always took place where there was much water. Jesus was baptized in the Jordan river, and 'came up immediately from the water' (Matt 3:16). John baptized in Aenon, near to Salim, 'because there was much water there' (John 3:23). When Philip baptized the eunuch, they 'went down into the water' (Acts 8:38) and 'came up out of the water' (v. 39).

3. *The proper motive for baptism.* The purpose of baptism is succinctly stated in 1 Peter 3:21. It is 'not the removal of the filth of the flesh, but the answer of a good conscience towards God'. Water on the body cannot cleanse sin in the heart. Only the blood of Christ can cleanse from sin, from a legal point of view (1 John 1:7). But baptism is connected with salvation symbolically. When Ananias said to Paul, 'Arise and be baptized, and wash away your sins, calling on the name of the Lord' (Acts 22:16), he did not mean that the baptism actually took away Paul's guilt. Either he meant that the baptism in *symbol* washed away his sins, or 'wash away your sins' refers to Paul's change of life following his baptism. If baptism were absolutely essential to salvation then the thief on the cross was not saved, contrary to what Christ specifically stated, and one could not be saved who through circumstantial hindrances could not be baptized. Baptismal regeneration was one of the first heresies to develop in the age following the apostles.

An alternate view

It is our view that baptism is for believers only, for the reasons just briefly cited. However, a great host of Christians holding to a high view of Scripture interpret the Bible to allow for the baptism of infants of Christian families. The primary argument for infant baptism (given, for example, by John Calvin in his *Institutes*) can be seen by a syllogism, which consists of a major premise, a minor premise, and a conclusion.

Major Premise: In the Abrahamic Covenant, continued in principle throughout the Old Testament period, male children were circumcized as a seal of the covenant.

Minor Premise: In the New Testament, baptism has taken the place of circumcision.

Conclusion: Infants are to be baptized as a seal of the covenant of grace.

Paedobaptists find support for this (see the footnotes to the *Westminster Confession of Faith*) in the fact that the 'households' of Lydia and the Philippian jailer (Acts 16:15; 16:31, 34) were baptized. This implies, in their view, that the children (even those unable to respond to the gospel) were included.

It is the minor premise in the syllogism that is in dispute. We deny that baptism has formally taken the place of circumcision, contending instead that circumcision was a part of a *typical* order of things, and that the antitype is regeneration, which comes to those who believe in Christ. Infant salvation, which we hope for based on the mercy of God, would be through God's sovereign good pleasure and is not connected in any way with a physical rite.

As far as the household salvation is concerned it should be noted that the household of the Philippian jailer who were baptized 'believed in God' (v. 34).

In their foundational documents Paedobaptists in the Reformed tradition contend that baptism for infants is a seal of the covenant of God, and connects them to the promises of God for salvation, though baptism does not *ipso facto* and formally save.

The Lord's Supper

On the occasion of our Lord's last observance of the Jewish Passover, just before his death, he instituted the Lord's Supper as a perpetual memorial in the church (Matt. 26:26-29; 1 Cor. 11:23-26). That this rite was to be continued can be seen from the fact that it was enjoined by the apostles and practised by the early church (Acts 2:42; Acts 20:7; 1 Cor. 10:16).

1. *Elements of the Lord's Supper*. There are two elements in Communion: bread and 'the fruit of the vine'. The bread used by Jesus was no doubt the unleavened bread of the Passover. Leaven in Scripture is a symbol of evil (1 Cor. 5:6-8). Some argue from this that the church should use unleavened bread, but the symbolism of the Lord's Supper does not especially stress the element of purity but communion with Christ. The beverage was the 'fruit of the vine', or grapes (Matt. 26:29). In the apostolic age there was no way of artificially preserving grape juice, so undoubtedly fermented wine was used. Unfortunately, the Corinthians were intoxicated at the Lord's Supper because some of them were abusing it (1 Cor. 11:21). The bread represents Christ's body, the wine his blood (Matt. 26:26, 28).

2. *The participants in the Lord's Supper*. Just as baptism is for believers only, so is the Lord's Supper. Jesus gave the command to share in Communion to his disciples, Christians. It is a family ordinance, not for outsiders. In his instructions to the church at Corinth, Paul states that the Lord's Supper is an expression of the believer's *communion* with his Lord

(1 Cor. 10:16). It also denotes the unity of Christians in 'one body' with their Lord (10:17). This certainly shows that it is for Christians only.

In the church of the New Testament, apparently all who took Communion had been baptized. Some argue from this that Communion is only for immersed believers. This was the prevailing view of Baptists until recent years, and was known as *closed Communion*. Non-baptized, that is non-immersed, Christians were not allowed to sit at the Lord's table. On the other hand, the question may be raised, if we can have spiritual fellowship with others than Baptists, should we not invite them to share a common faith at the Lord's table? This question has been debated and will continue to be, no doubt. (Our own church has a policy of open Communion.)

3. *The host of the Lord's Supper.* Is Communion a private act of worship between any group of believers, including those in a family, or is it for the church alone? Propriety seems to indicate that it should be served in the church. Yet sometimes believers cannot come to church, through illness, etc. Wherever Communion is enjoyed, it should be with dignity and solemnity. Paul warns about turning it into a common meal (1 Cor. 11:22).

4. *The purpose of the Lord's Supper*

a. *Negatively*

- It is not to convey salvation. Those who believe the Lord's Supper is a sacrament feel that it communicates or 'seals' salvation. This is not true any more than wearing a wedding ring makes a person married.
- It is not a re-enactment of Calvary. Catholics teach *transubstantiation*, the view that, by a miracle, the bread

becomes the body of Christ and the wine becomes the blood of Christ. But 'this is my body' means 'this is a symbol of my body'. Hebrews 12:29 says, 'God is a consuming fire.' Does this mean that he is a literal fire? Obviously not. The doctrine of the mass not only means that partakers of Communion are cannibals but if the wine is the literal blood of Jesus, then Calvary is repeated, which is blasphemous.

- The purpose of the Lord's Supper is not to sit in judgement on the piety of others. Those who participate are told to examine themselves, not others (1 Cor. 11:28). Of course it is the responsibility of the church to warn against the participation of those who are not converted or walking with the Lord.

b. *Positively*, what is the purpose of the Lord's Supper? It is a festal, commemorative celebration of our Lord's redemptive achievements and our participation in them. It is a *preaching ordinance*, in that it proclaims the gospel in symbol. It is *personal* in that it speaks of the believer's faith.

- It symbolizes Christ's death for our sins (1 Cor. 11:26). In Mark 14:24 Jesus says, 'This is my blood of the new covenant, which is shed for many.'

- It symbolizes the believer's union with Christ. 1 Corinthians 10:17 says, 'For we, though many, are one bread and one body; for we all partake of that one bread.'

- It symbolizes the continual dependence of the Christian on the crucified one (1 Cor. 10:16). Baptism shows how

Calvary delivers us once for all from sin. Communion shows how the blood continues to cleanse.

The Lord's Supper is a *link with the past* (what Christ did for us), *a lesson for the present* (his present ministry to us), and a *look into the future*: 'You proclaim the Lord's death till he comes' (1 Cor. 11:26).

Purity and discipline of the church

The Christian is commanded to love all men (1 Thess. 3:12) and live peaceably with all men (Rom. 12:18). But believers have a special relationship with each other, which excludes outsiders. A church fellowship is a narrower circle even within Christian fellowship, *it is a covenant body*. This principle is illustrated in human love. Human love can extend to all men, our neighbours and others as well. But in marriage there is a covenant arrangement.

Just as there are grounds for establishing Christian and church fellowship, there are grounds for breaking it. God wants the church to be a special holy body (see 2 Cor. 6:14-18). The church should, ideally, consist only of truly converted people.

Though perfection is not possible in this life, we should strive for it. Christians are to strive for perfect obedience to the Lord (1 John 2:1). Yet that is never possible in this life (1 John 1:8). Even so, God does not want unbelievers in the church, yet even in the churches during the apostolic period, some did filter in. Judas was not saved. It is doubtful that Ananias and Sapphira (Acts 5:1-11) and Simon Magus (Acts 8:14-25) had truly come to the Lord. Diotrephes was a church member (3 John 9), as was Jezebel (Rev. 2:20). But the church should not passively allow such people to harm the church. Their evil influence should be stopped.

Grounds for church discipline

Ephesians 5:11 says, 'Have no fellowship with the unfruitful works of darkness, but rather expose them.'

1. *The heretical* (Rom. 16:17; Titus 3:10; 2 John 10-11). In the last passage, house seems to refer to the church house, not the place of dwelling.

2. *The immoral* (see 1 Cor. 5:4-7). This was a case of incest (see also 2 Thess. 3:11-15).

Measures of discipline

Sometimes, in extreme cases, expulsion is necessary. Should a person, such as the incestuous man at Corinth, be allowed to come and fellowship with the saints, and participate in church activities when he openly lives in sin? No. Paul says, 'Purge out the old leaven' (1 Cor. 5:7). Normally such people would leave on their own accord; but not always.

1. The purity of the church is an important consideration (1 Cor. 5:6).

2. We should seek the *good* of the offender (1 Cor. 5:5). To ignore a problem can sometimes be harmful; rebuke is necessary.

Spirit of discipline

Rebuke or correction should be done in love and humility (Gal. 6:1; 2 Thess. 3:15).

8.
Learning about the future

A surprisingly large portion of the Bible is taken up with *prophecy*. Of this, much yet remains to be fulfilled. The future of the *righteous*, the future of the *wicked*, and the future of the *earth* are all spoken of in Scripture. Since what we believe about what lies ahead for the universe and mankind affects how we live now, it is important that we study Bible prophecy. We will deal with this subject under five headings: the intermediate state, the second coming of Christ, the latter-day glory, the judgement, and heaven and hell.

The intermediate state

Like other subjects, the subject of death, the place of departed spirits etc., receives an increase of light in the progress of biblical revelation. The New Testament brings into clarity what was hinted at in the Old Testament.

The place of the dead in the Old Testament

The Old Testament Scriptures spoke of all the dead as going to a place known as *sheol*. This word is translated 'hell' thirty-one times, 'grave' thirty-one times, and 'pit' three times (AV).

System of Bible doctrine

Its meaning, in short, is 'the place of the dead'. It is the place where both the righteous (Gen. 42:38) and the wicked go (Deut. 32:22; Prov. 9:18). From the standpoint of earthly activity, everything comes to a halt in *sheol* (Ps. 6:5). But there are Old Testament indications of consciousness, for the soul dwells there (Ps. 16:10). Isaiah 14:9 says, 'The grave (*sheol*) below is all astir to meet you at your coming; it rouses the spirits of the departed to greet you...' (NIV).

A gleam of hope is held out for the righteous for deliverance from death and the grave (Prov. 14:32; Ps. 16:10; Hosea 13:14). In fact, there is no indication that the righteous suffered in *sheol*. This raises the possibility of *two compartments* in *sheol*, one for the righteous and one for the wicked. According to the *Imperial Bible Dictionary*, this was an idea 'entertained by the ancients' (article on Hades). This is seemingly confirmed by the New Testament where the word *Hades*, meaning 'place of the dead or departed spirits', takes the place of *sheol*. In the story of the rich man and Lazarus (Luke 16:19-31) the former is represented as going to Hades and he sees the righteous beggar afar off in 'Abraham's bosom'.

The place of the dead in the New Testament

A very clear distinction is made in the New Testament as to where the wicked and the righteous go. The wicked go to Hades or hell, a prison for their departed spirits (same as *sheol* of the Old Testament). It appears eleven times, translated 'hell' ten times, and 'grave' (1 Cor. 15:55) once. (Modern editors of the Greek New Testament do not include Hades in this verse but read death [*thanatos*] twice.) The book of Revelation shows clearly what Hades is now. According to Revelation 1:18 Jesus now has the keys of Hades and death. This means he controls the realm of the departed wicked and the grave where their bodies are, indicated by the two words Hades and death. Revelation 20:13-14 tell us what happens to the wicked at their resurrection. Hades delivers up her prisoners, the souls of sinners, they are joined to their bodies and cast into the lake of fire.

On the other hand the righteous go into the immediate presence of God (Phil. 1:23; 2 Cor. 5:6-8). Hebrews 12:23 states that the spirits of just men are now made perfect. This is a much more joyful prospect than the shadowy *sheol* of the Old Testament saints. Did a change take place in the location of saints between the Old Testament and New Testament periods? Many think so, including myself. In refering to Hades the *Imperial Bible Dictionary* says, 'by the personal work and mediation of Christ the whole church of God rose to a higher condition'. This is partly based on Acts 2:27. Peter connects David's statement 'For you will not leave my soul in Hades' with the resurrection of Christ. Christ certainly did not stay in the 'realms of the dead', and David himself seems to teach that Christ's resurrection would ensure his departure from *sheol*. Furthermore, Ephesians 4:8-9 supports the idea that Jesus led the Old Testament believers into the presence of God at his ascension. First he descended into the lower parts of the earth (he died) and then he ascended on high leading captivity captive (see Ps. 68:18). The intimation seems to be that Jesus went to *sheol* or Hades, liberated the Old Testament believers from that place, and when he ascended took them with him to the presence of God.

The second coming of Jesus

Of course any dramatic intervention of God in the affairs of men and nations is a 'coming'. Christ warned the church at Ephesus that he might 'come' and take away the candlestick

(Rev. 2:5). This is a coming in temporal judgement. Jesus said to the disciples, 'I will not leave you orphans; I will come to you' (John 14:18). This was fulfilled spiritually in the coming of the Spirit on Pentecost. Jesus once said to the disciples, 'For assuredly, I say to you, you will not have gone through the cities of Israel before the Son of Man comes' (Matt. 10:23). Obviously this refers to a visitation of Jesus soon to happen. But there is a final coming of Christ at the end of this age.

Characteristics of Christ's second coming

1. *Literal and physical* (Acts 1:11). Jesus' ascension was bodily and physical, and the angel said that his return would be 'in like manner' (see Matt. 25:31; John 14:3; Phil. 3:20; and Heb. 9:28).

2. *Visible*. Revelation 1:7 says, 'Behold, he is coming with clouds, and every eye will see him, even they who pierced him.'

3. *Extended*. The word 'coming' can be used in two different senses. Sometimes it means a single isolated event. 'I expect the coming of Horace at any moment now.' But it can also be used in the sense of what is equivalent to a visitation. 'We are looking forward to the coming of Aunt Emily next week.' In this sense 'coming' could last an extended period of time. In my opinion, all the events that are associated with the coming of Christ cannot be collected into *one* event taking a short period of time. These include the translation of believers (1 Thess. 4:17), the resurrection of dead believers (1 Cor. 15:51-52), the judgement of the living and the dead (2 Tim. 4:1), and the destruction of the earth (2 Peter 3:10). Will all these things take place at once, that is, in a brief period of time? I

do not think so; certainly not if we believe in a 'latter-day glory' period preceded by his coming.

The purpose of Christ's coming

We believe that Jesus Christ will return literally and physically to do business with men *directly* here on earth. During this extended period of time, or in connection with it, the following events (and more, no doubt) will take place.

1. *The resurrection of dead believers and the rapture of living ones* (1 Thess. 4:13-18). Paul says here that those living on earth when Jesus comes must wait for believers in the grave to rise up and go before them. Then the Lord will 'transform' our vile or 'lowly' body, one that is affected by sin, and give us one like his 'glorious body' (Phil. 3:21). Then the Christian will physically 'see' his Lord, and 'be like him' (1 John 3:2).

In 1 Corinthians 15, Paul discusses at length the subject of the resurrection. He says that Jesus rose from the dead as the 'firstfruits' of those who 'have fallen asleep' or are dead in Christ (v. 20). The resurrection of believers is assured by the triumph of Christ over the grave. Paul draws a vivid contrast between the body that died and the one that is raised. It is sown in corruption, and raised in incorruption (v. 42). It is sown in dishonour, and raised in glory (v. 43). It is sown in weakness, it is raised in power (v. 43). It is sown a natural body, it is raised a spiritual body (v. 44). The resurrected, glorified body of the saints will be free from sin, pain and weakness of any kind. Death will be swallowed up in victory (v. 54).

Aside from the resurrection and the rapture, the Bible connects the coming of Christ with the following points. Rather than discuss these events in detail, we will merely mention them and defer more detailed evaluation.

2. *The destruction of the 'man of sin' sometimes called Antichrist.* He is the same as the 'little horn' of Daniel 7:8, 11 and 21. He makes war with the saints and prevails against them, 'until the Ancient of Days came' (Dan. 7:22). He is called the 'man of sin' in 2 Thessalonians 2:3 and is destroyed 'with the brightness of his coming' (2:8).

3. *The conversion of the Jews.* The future conversion of Israel is predicted in the Old and New Testaments (see Jer. 31:31-34; Rom. 11:25-32). *When?* The answers seem to be given in Zechariah 12:10-14. The Spirit of grace and supplications will be given to the inhabitants of Jerusalem when 'they look upon me whom they have pierced'. A physical sight of Jesus does not convert anyone, but conversion can happen at the same time as a physical glimpse when the Holy Spirit gives spiritual sight.

4. *Judgement.* Paul states that Jesus will *judge* the living and the dead at his appearing and his kingdom (2 Tim. 4:1). This accords with what he told the Athenians, namely that Jesus would 'judge the world in righteousness' (Acts 17:31). Essentially, to judge means to bring character to the test and assign rewards and punishment based on character.

a. *The believers or righteous will be judged.* Romans 14:10 says, 'For we shall all stand before the judgement seat of Christ.' The same sentiment appears in 2 Corinthians 5:10. Then the righteous character of Christians will be manifested and proclaimed. The parable of the talents implies that when Jesus returns he will evaluate his people based on how they used their 'talents' or the things entrusted to them (Matt. 25:14-30). Their sins cannot condemn them, however, for they are forgiven through Christ's atonement.

b. *The wicked shall be judged.* Whereas believers will not be punished for their sins because Christ paid the price for them, the unsaved will stand before Christ to 'receive a just reward' for their sins against God (Heb. 2:2). Revelation 20:11-15 gives a picture of a 'great white throne' with Jesus sitting upon it. The dead, small and great all stand before God. Every man is judged according to his works. Then the wicked will be cast into hell (v. 14).

5. *The establishment of worldwide peace and righteousness.* Perhaps the most dramatic portrayal of the coming of Jesus is in Revelation 19:11-16. He is seen as coming on a white steed, wearing many crowns, with eyes as a flame of fire. Known here as 'Faithful and True', the Son of God comes to judge and make war (v. 11). Verse 15 says that he will strike the nations and rule them with a rod of iron. Then the kingdoms of this world will 'become the kingdoms of our Lord and of his Christ' (11:15). What conditions will be like for this age, lasting 1000 years according to Revelation 20, is also described in the Hebrew prophets, particularly Isaiah.

6. *The destruction of the earth.* Peter predicts that in the last days there will be scoffers who will ask, 'Where is the promise of his coming?' (2 Peter 3:3-4). Then he says that God will certainly fulfil his promise to send his Son, though he does not act in a hurry, for with God one day is as a thousand years (v. 8). The apostle Peter comes then to this notable event. 'But the day of the Lord will come as a thief in the night, in which the heavens will pass away with a great noise, and the elements will melt with fervent heat; both the earth and the works that are in it will be burned up' (2 Peter 3:10). This obviously follows the millennium. Then the earth will be destroyed.

The latter-day glory

The Bible teaches that before the final state of man and the earth is ushered in there will be a time of universal peace, righteousness and salvation. This is predicted in the Old Testament and confirmed in the New.

Preliminary events before the 'latter-day glory'

The age we are now living in will evidently end in apostasy and judgement. There will be a worldwide conspiracy against God headed by 'the man of sin'. The book of Daniel and Revelation are specific about these things.

1. *Daniel's outline of Jewish history.* In Daniel 9:24-27 God's programme for the end times is given. It centres around the Jewish people. Verse 24 says, 'Seventy weeks are determined for your people and for your holy city.' Days in this period refers to years, so 490 years are in view. At the beginning of the 490 years there was a commandment to rebuild Jerusalem in 'troublesome times' (v. 25). A commonly accepted date is 445 B. C. when Artaxerxes the Persian monarch commissioned Nehemiah to complete the reconstruction of the city. The passage reveals that after 483 weeks the Messiah would come (v. 25). Sir Robert Anderson calculated that 69 prophetic years of 360 days would bring the calendar to 6 April A. D. 32, or the 10th Nison, which was the day of Jesus' triumphal entry. According to verse 26 there is a gap after the first sixty-nine weeks, for Messiah is cut off and the city and sanctuary are destroyed by the people of 'the Prince who is to come'. Jerusalem was invaded and finally destroyed by the Romans in A. D. 70. During the final week or seven years, the Prince makes a covenant with Israel but soon brings desolation and abominations (v. 27). We believe this refers to the

work of Antichrist, during the final seven years of Daniel's 490, yet future.

2. *The tribulation period.* Daniel 12:1 says, 'There shall be a time of trouble, such as never was since there was a nation...' Jeremiah 30:7 calls it the time of Jacob's trouble. Jesus prophesied: 'For then there will be a great tribulation, such as has not been since the beginning of the world until this time, no, nor ever shall be' (Matt. 24:21). Based on the fact that the Antichrist will break his covenant with Israel in the midst of the week, it would seem that this period will be the last half of the final seven-year period or three and a half years. The same time span is referred to in Daniel 7:25; Revelation 11:2; 12:6, 14; and 13:5. It is generally thought that Revelation 6 - 19 describes in highly figurative language some of the events of this period. According to chapter 6, there will be war, famine, death and anarchy on earth.

3. *This will be the period when 'the man of sin' (Antichrist) is in power.* In Daniel 7:8, 21 and 24 he is called the 'little horn' rising from the ten horns of the revived Roman Empire. In 2 Thessalonians 2:3, he is called the man of sin and in 2:8, 'the lawless one'. In Revelation 13 he is pictured as a beast coming out of the earth. There are actually two beasts mentioned here. Some think the second (13:11-18) is the Antichrist and the first (13:1-10) is the political system which gives him his power (v. 12).

4. *The Antichrist will persecute the saints.* Daniel 7:21 says that the Antichrist will make war with the saints and prevail against them. This idea is repeated in Revelation 13:7. Revelation 20:4 tells us that among the participants in the 'first resurrection' are those who were martyred because they would not submit to his rule. This shows us that believers

will go through the tribulation period. Thus the first resurrection is after the tribulation period. Revelation 20 plainly
indicates that there will be a resurrection after the tribulation,
and Daniel 12:2 teaches the same thing. Jesus taught in
Matthew 24:29-31 that the rapture will be after the tribulation
period (see v. 29), for then Jesus will 'gather together his elect
from the four winds'. It is also interesting to note that Paul
teaches that the second coming of Jesus and the translation
of the saints will come at the 'last trumpet' (1 Cor. 15:52). But
in the book of Revelation the trumpets are sounding during
the tribulation period and it is at the last trumpet that the
kingdoms of this world become the kingdoms of Jesus (Rev.
11:15).

Based on this evidence we must conclude that the rapture
is not an occurrence separated from the second coming but
is one of the events (the resurrection of dead believers will
precede it) attending Jesus' descent to the earth to judge the
wicked and reward the righteous. We conclude from biblical
evidence, therefore, that the first resurrection and the rapture will be accomplished by the visible return of the Lord in
glory and will inaugurate the latter-day glory. Actually, if the
resurrection of dead believers and the rapture are before the
tribulation, then there will not be two resurrections as taught
by Revelation 20 but *three*: one *before* the tribulation, when
all the dead believers prior to the second coming are raised;
one *after* the tribulation when the saints killed by Antichrist
will be raised; and finally the 'second resurrection' (alluded
to in Rev. 20:5), but amended by pretribulationists to be the
'third resurrection'.

5. *Israel and the latter-day glory*. All the events mentioned
before as being preliminary to the latter-day glory involve
Israel. Daniel's seventy weeks pertain primarily to Israel. The
tribulation period is the time of 'Jacob's trouble'. It is with

Israel that the Antichrist enters into covenant and it is they whom he persecutes. Perhaps it would be helpful here to review some of the teachings of Scripture relating to Israel in 'the latter days'.

a. *Events on 'Israel's Calendar'.* Jesus prophesied the destruction of the temple (Matt. 24:2). Luke 21:20-24 describe the invasion of the Romans under Vespasion in A. D. 68. Following this, as Jesus clearly explained, Israel is to be scattered throughout all nations. 'And they will fall by the edge of the sword, and be led away captive into all nations' (Luke 21:24). Isaiah 11:12 speaks of the dispersion of Judah through the 'four corners of the earth'.

b. *Israel's blindness.* Because Israel rejected her Messiah, God has given her up to spiritual and judicial blindness. This blindness will last till 'the fulness of the Gentiles has come in' (see Rom. 11:25). Paul speaks of this judicial hardening as a veil upon the hearts of the Israelites, a veil that will eventually be taken away (2 Cor. 3:13-16).

c. *Israel's return.* The Old Testament prophesies Israel's return to their homeland, and the New Testament confirms this. Ezekiel 36:24 says, 'For I will take you from among the nations, gather you out of all countries, and bring you into your own land.' We have seen this partially fulfilled in our own day. Since in the initial stage the return is in God's anger (Ezek. 22:20), we assume this first gathering is in unbelief. Interestingly, the Zionist movement which initiated the modern reconstruction of Israel was not generated on Christian premises but was merely a desire for Jews to reclaim their homeland. The economic reconstruction of Israel is seen in Amos 9:14-15. Notice that 'no longer shall they be pulled up', which shows that the return under

Zerubbabel is not in view here. The second temple which
was built under this leader was destroyed by the Romans.
Another literally fulfilled event is the perpetual enmity of
the Arabs against Israel, described in Ezekiel 35:1-6.

d. *Final war against Israel.* There was a time when the section of the world known as the Middle East had little
   international importance. Palestine was a wasteland where
   Bedouin tribes wandered. Two things have changed this.
   The first thing is the Zionist movement, which brought
   Jews from all over the world streaming back to Israel
   following its re-establishment as a nation in 1948. The
   second thing is the crucial importance of petroleum for
   the industrialized world. Richard Nixon, a former president of the United States of America, once said that the
   nation that controls the Middle East will have Europe by
   the throat. World attention is now focused on Israel and
   her Arab neighbours. Passages such as Zechariah 8:20-
   23 indicate that Jerusalem will become the religious centre
   of the earth. She will also become an international sore
   spot, called in Zechariah 12:2 a 'cup of drunkenness', to
   surrounding peoples and in verse 3 a 'very heavy stone'.
   Ultimately, according to Zechariah 14:2, 'all the nations'
   will be mustered against this tiny kingdom. This will
   certainly signal the near advent of Jesus for, immediately
   after, it says that the Lord will go forth and 'fight against
   those nations' (v. 3). Then Jesus will come and his feet
   will stand upon the Mount of Olives where he often stood
   and taught during his first advent (v. 4). Perhaps this is
   the same as the gigantic attack upon Christ mentioned in
   Revelation 19:19. When Jesus comes he will not only rescue Israel but will also totally overthrow the beast or Antichrist system (Rev. 19:20). This event will bring the world
   to the long anticipated time known as 'the millennium'.

Characteristics of the latter-day glory

Will there be a period of universal peace and righteousness upon the earth before the 'final solution' of heaven and hell come about? Consider the following biblical data as proof that there will be such a time. In the vision of Nebuchadnezzar, interpreted by Daniel, *a fifth kingdom* emerges which fills the whole earth (Dan. 2:35). In various places in the Old Testament it is said that all nations will eventually serve the Messiah. Psalm 22:27 says that all the ends of the world shall turn to the Lord. Jesus was the antitype of Solomon, whom all nations shall serve (Ps. 72:11; see also Dan. 7:14, 27). The time is coming is when 'the earth shall be full of the knowledge of the LORD as the waters cover the sea' (Isa. 11:9). At that time there will be no need of mission work for all shall know the Lord from the least to the greatest (Jer. 31:34).

1. Then *Jesus and his people will reign* in a more visible form over the earth. Jesus now rules over the entire universe at the right hand of God, but when he returns he will put down all opposition and rule with a rod of iron (Rev. 19:15). According to Revelation 5:10 the redeemed will rule with him on the earth. An interesting point is raised by Luke 22:30 where Jesus asserted that the apostles would sit on thrones judging the twelve tribes of Israel. The apostles will have, evidently, a special place in the visible kingdom of Christ. But all Christians, including the martyrs, will reign with Jesus (Rev. 20:4, 6).

2. *Jerusalem will be the spiritual headquarters* of the world. The conversion of Israel has already been alluded to. After the Lord comes to destroy the nations gathered against Israel (Zech. 14:3) and he becomes 'King over all the earth' (v. 9) all nations will go up to Jerusalem to worship. There are

difficulties, of course, in taking these passages literally. Will such Jewish feasts as 'the Feast of Tabernacles' (v. 16) be restored? Either this is symbolic of the spiritual worship consistent with the gospel of redemption or some literal commemoration will be set up, which will not, of course, reverse the impact of Christ's atonement. The book of Hebrews clearly teaches that Jesus fulfilled the types and ceremonies of the Old Testament. In the light of Isaiah 2:3, which says that the law shall 'go forth' out of Zion, we believe that Jesus, with his ancient people Israel now confirmed in a saving relationship to him, will bring the world to faith in himself.

3. *Satan will be bound* and his influence curtailed, eliminated in fact, during this period. In Revelation 20:1 we are told that John saw an angel come down from heaven with a chain in his hand. He laid hold of Satan and bound him a thousand years, casting him into the bottomless pit. This interesting pronouncement is given of Satan: '...so that he should deceive the nations no more till the thousand years were finished' (v. 3). Satan, of course, is the most powerful evil force in the universe, the tempter, enemy and destroyer of man. He is the 'god of this world' and he wages a fierce war against God. What would happen if his influence ceased? The millennium will tell. Incidentally, here in Revelation 20, we have the only intimation of how long the latter-day glory will last: a thousand years. If we were to apply the day-year principle to this period (a possibility, to say the least), it will last 360,000 years.

4. The latter-day glory will be *a time of universal peace and righteousness*. Men from time immemorial have dreamed of a time when war will cease and people will live in peace. Such a time will come, but not by means devised by men. God will bring it about in his time and in his way. Isaiah speaks of a

period when men will destroy instruments of war (2:4). During this period, even the beasts of the earth will lose their ferocity (Isa. 11:6). Also, with the peoples of the world in a converted state and with Satan bound, righteousness will prevail. Then the world will be filled with the knowledge of the glory of the Lord (Hab. 2:14). They shall neither 'hurt nor destroy' in that day (Isa. 11:9), in other words, violence will be unknown. What a glorious time this will be! And to think, all Christians of all ages and the saints of the Old Testament will share in these blessings.

5. The latter-day glory will be *a time of material prosperity and happiness.* Isaiah 65:18-25 seems to describe conditions during this period. Some of the elements are joy (v. 19), longevity of life (v. 20), fruitful and successful labour (vv. 21-23) and speedy answers to prayer (v. 24).

Termination of the latter-day glory

Revelation 20:7-10 indicates that following the millennium Satan will be liberated again for a brief period of time. He is able to muster one last great assault upon the saints of God and succeeds even in encircling them (v. 9). But then fire from heaven falls and consumes this evil and hostile aggregation of people led by Satan, and he is summarily dispatched to the lake of fire where the Antichrist forces had already been confined for 1000 years (v. 10). Thus ends once and for all the long and dreadful reign of the devil.

Alternate views on the millennium

The view on the millennium advocated in this book is known as premillennialism, meaning that Jesus will come before the

millennium, or the thousand-year reign. This view was held
by many of the church fathers, a few Puritans, and Christian
leaders such as John Gill, Horatious and Andrew Bonar,
J. C. Ryle, C. H. Spurgeon, and in our own time Francis
Schaeffer and Gordon Clark.

There are two other views held by orthodox believers who
hold to a high view of Scripture.

A-millennialism

A-millennialism contends that there will be no period of universal peace and righteousness prior to the final development
of God's kingdom in heaven. Those of this school stress that
the book of Revelation is largely symbolic and portrays not
so much literal historical events but the ongoing struggle
between Jesus Christ and Satan. The thousand-year passage
in the book of Revelation is not to be taken literally, but refers
to the gospel era in which, comparatively speaking, Satan has
been bound by Christ's triumphant work and the mission of
the church.

The prophecies of the Old Testament that relate to Israel
are fulfilled in the church and there is no specific plan of God
for the nation Israel other than that which all believers share.
The 'Israel of God' (Gal. 6:16) refers to believers. They point
to New Testament passages such as Acts 15:16 which, in their
view, teaches that the conversion of the Gentiles fulfils the
Old Testament promise that the tabernacle of David would
be rebuilt.

Postmillennialism

Postmillennialists (contending that Christ will come after the
millennium), like the premillennialists, believe that before
the final triumph of the kingdom of God in heaven the visible

kingdom of Christ will prevail over the earth. They do not believe that this will come about through the literal Second Coming (they do not deny that this will happen eventually) but will be accomplished through the ministry of the church and great effusions of the Spirit of God. Evangelical post-millennialism, which stresses all the great truths of orthodox Christianity, is not to be confused with the liberal view which teaches that the world will be Christianized through education, social reform and political activism. Postmillennialism relies heavily on the texts of the Hebrew prophets, which predict worldwide triumph for the Messiah's kingdom, which they believe will culminate the present age of grace. In its best form it infused a spirit of optimism and hope in missions, since it envisioned that the gospel would indeed prevail over evil prior to the termination of history as we now know it. Both the a-millennial and postmillennial positions adhere to a general resurrection of men, as opposed to the premillennial view, which seems to separate resurrections.

Errors of dispensationalism

Although there are no doubt elements of dispensationalism in all systems of eschatology (the study of things relating to the end of time), we believe that three significant errors are inherent in the type of premillennialism which has been popularized by such books as the *Scofield Reference Bible*.

1. *A radical distinction between Israel and the church.* High dispensationalists contend that believers of the Old Covenant period are not in the church of Jesus Christ. It is our view, however, that the church for which Jesus died (Eph. 5:25) embraces all the redeemed of all ages and that the Old Testament believers are a part of the 'things in heaven' which Jesus reconciled when he died on Calvary (Col. 1:20).

2. *A misconception of the mission of Jesus to earth.* High dispensationalists contend that Jesus Christ came to earth 2000 years ago to restore the earthly kingdom to the nation of Israel. In this view the kingdom referred to in the Gospels (Matthew to John) as being 'at hand' was rejected by Israel and as a result Jesus went to the cross and died for sinners. Jesus will come again some day and fulfil what he failed to do the first time. Many believe that the 'kingdom' teachings of the Gospels relate to Israel and cannot apply to believers.

3. *Separating the rapture from the second coming of Jesus.* There is no evidence in the New Testament that the translation of the saints, or rapture, is a separate event from the literal, visible coming of Jesus. The Bible plainly teaches that as Jesus is on the way back to this planet to judge men and nations he will first raise the dead believers, and then 'catch up' the saints living on earth and transform them, before returning with them to triumph over Antichrist. The notion that the rapture is an event seven years before Jesus comes has produced, particularly in America, a kind of escapist mentality. Believers in the days of the apostles expected to face tribulation and suffering in this world, not escape from it.

The final resurrection and judgement

In Revelation 20:11-15 a solemn judgement scene is portrayed. An awesome being sits on a great white throne 'from whose face the earth and the heaven fled away' (v. 11). In the light of Acts 17:31, we believe that this personage is Jesus Christ, the one appointed to 'judge the world in righteousness'. On this occasion the 'dead', small and great stand before God (Rev. 20:12). After the judgement, the wicked ones are cast into hell (v. 14). This scene relates to two important realities: the second resurrection and the judgement.

The second resurrection

As is seen by Revelation 20:6, there was a 'first resurrection' before the millennium. Included in this are all the believers who died before Christ's second coming, including those who were put to death by the Antichrist (v. 4). The teaching is that the *wicked dead* will not be raised till after the millennium. Verse 5 says, 'But the rest of the dead did not live again until the thousand years were finished.' Thus we learn that the wicked of history will be raised after the 'latter-day glory'.

This raises an interesting question. What about the righteous who died during the millennium? For at least a thousand years the world will be populated largely with righteous people. Although we have reason to believe the longevity of life will be greatly increased then, we have no reason to think that there will be no death. So either believers who died during this period will be transformed immediately upon death and given new bodies, or else they will sleep in the earth till the end of the millennium. My own opinion (many premillennialists would disagree with me on this) is that the righteous who died during the millennium will be included in the 'second resurrection'. It is noteworthy that while Revelation 20:5 says that the 'rest of the dead' did not live again till the millennium is over, it does not say specifically that this group includes only the wicked. John 5:28-29 seems to point to a future general resurrection, when all in the graves will come forth, some to the resurrection of life and some to the resurrection of condemnation. My belief is that this will be after the millennium.

The judgement

Paul teaches clearly that when Jesus comes for his people, they will stand before him at the judgement seat (2 Cor. 5:10). But this judgement will, comparatively speaking, include few people: only those who were converted before the latter-day glory. It will not include the unrighteous in history nor will it include the people who were saved during the millennium. Thus there must still (that is, after the millennium) be a judgement of all the wicked and, in fact, many righteous people. This, in our opinion, is what will constitute the 'general judgement'. This is what the hymn refers to when it says,

> There's a great day coming, a great day coming,
> There's a great day coming by and by;
> When the saints and the sinners will be parted right and
> left.

Is this the judgement day spoken of in Matthew 25:31-46? Since on this occasion the wicked are sent immediately into everlasting punishment, we believe it is. Some, however, feel that the 'sheep and goats' judgement will be a judgement of nations at Jesus' second coming, before the millennium.

We will now sum up briefly what we believe about the final judgement.

1. *The subjects of the final judgement.* First, it is clear that all men will be judged eventually, one time or another. Hebrews 9:27 says, 'And as it is appointed for men to die once, but after this the judgement...' All the righteous prior to Christ's second coming will be judged at the time of his coming. All those saved after Christ's coming, and all the wicked of history, will be judged (in my opinion) at the end of the millennium.

But the final judgement will also include the sinful angels (see 2 Peter 2:4; and Jude 6). The righteous angels will not be judged but will be attendants at the judgement (Matt. 13:41-42; 25:31).

2. *The judge.* According to Hebrews 12:23, God is the 'Judge of all'. But his judicial activity at the last day, as well as at present, is exercised through Jesus Christ (John 5:22; Acts 17:31).

3. *The purpose of the final judgement.* It is not *discovery*, for the Lord already knows who his people are (2 Tim. 2:19). But rather it is to dispense rewards and punishment based on conduct (Ps. 62:12; Rom. 2:6). We should not forget that while the righteous are not saved because of their good works, their works are an evidence that they are saved and they will constitute the grounds of their Lord's approval (not acceptance) at the final judgement (Matt. 25:34-40).

4. *The basis of the final judgement.* On what grounds will people be judged? The only place where God's will is completely made known is in the Bible, which contains both the law and the gospel. This will be the basis of judgement. Jesus said, 'The word that I have spoken will judge him in the last day' (John 12:48). Revelation 20:12 mentions that the 'books' will be opened on this awesome and solemn occasion. Perhaps this will include the Lamb's Book of Life, containing the list of the saved, the book of the Scripture, and also the book of God's record of men's deeds.

Certainly the judgement of God will include such things as the degree of light a person has and the amount of opportunity. Those who have not heard the gospel will be judged by the light of nature and their consciences in which God's will is dimly made known (Rom. 1:19; 2:15). More severe punishment will await those who sin against the clear light of the gospel (Matt. 11:22, 24), and a special and fearful measure of justice will be meted on those who professed to follow Christ but turned away from him (Heb. 10:29).

The final states of the saved and unsaved

Thus far we have discussed a number of interesting subjects pertaining to that which is future, such as the second coming of Christ, the latter-day glory, the Antichrist, the tribulation period, the resurrections and judgement, etc. All of these are preparatory to God's final disposition of all accountable creatures. Eventually men will be judged as fitting into one of two categories, the saved and the unsaved, the righteous and the unrighteous. In this state they will remain for ever.

Heaven, the final home of the righteous

That the righteous would eventually enter into a place of happiness is dimly hinted at in the Old Testament (Isa. 25:8), but is clearly promised in the New Testament (Rev. 21:1-4).

1. *Heaven is a literal place.* Jesus spoke of heaven as a place (John 14:2, 4). It is no dreamy, unreal and imaginary concept. This means that it has real physical existence and dimensions. It is not a 'Beautiful Isle of Somewhere' but the blessed abode of the redeemed with their Lord. This is evident from the fact that the saints will have real bodies, just as Christ did when he arose from the dead. This place will include a new renovated earth (Rom. 8:19-23; 2 Peter 3:12-13), as following the judgement our present earth will be destroyed by fire.

2. *Heaven is a place of eternal happiness.* Through conversion men are in this life partially restored to the goal for which they were originally created: personal satisfaction and communion with God. Heaven will bring the work to completion. It is a place where there is no pain (Rev. 21:4), death (21:4), or any kind of sorrow. Although there will be activity, the

unpleasant aspects of earthly work will be removed, thus it is a place of rest (14:13).

3. *Heaven is a place of holiness.* There can be no unrighteousness in that place. Revelation 21:27 says, 'But there shall by no means enter it anything that defiles, or causes an abomination or a lie, but only those who are written in the Lamb's Book of Life.' The relationship of redeemed sinners with God will be fulfilled in the three realities of communion with God (21:3), worship of God (19:1), and service to God (22:3).

4. *Heaven is the final stage of God's plan of salvation for his people.* In the sense of justification the saved already have eternal life, but in the sense of glorification, they do not. Thus entering into heaven is, from one point of view, entering into eternal life (Matt. 25:46) and salvation (Rom. 13:11). Deliverance from the *penalty* and *power* of sin are in this life; deliverance from the *presence* of sin is in the next (1 Peter 1:5).

5. *Heaven is the climax of a pattern of activity begun in this life.* Romans 6:22 says, 'But now having been set free from sin, and having become slaves of God, you have your fruit to holiness, and the end, everlasting life.' No one will go to heaven who has not lived a holy life. The righteous will experience nothing, morally, in heaven which they have not had a sample of here. When Jesus comes he will *reward* every man according to his works (Matt. 16:27). Heaven will not be a reward based on merit, but a blessing based on obedience. Will there be degrees in heaven? I agree with Louis Berkhof who said, 'It is also evident from Scripture that there will be degrees in the bliss of heaven, Dan. 12:3; II Cor. 9:6... Notwithstanding this, however, the joy of each individual will be perfect and full.'[11]

6. *Heaven will be a place of progress.* In his *Manual of Systematic Theology* Alvah Hovey says of heaven, 'This blessedness will be forever increasing. For the soul will be restored to its normal condition, ever adding to its knowledge, and thereby to its happiness.'[12]

Hell, the final state of the unrighteous

Just as there will be an eternal habitation for the righteous, so there will be for the unrighteous. The Bible makes this plain.

1. *Hell is a literal place.* As discussed in the section on the intermediate state, there are two words for hell in the New Testament, *Hades* and *Gehenna*. To summarize, Hades corresponds to the Old Testament word *sheol*, which means 'place of the dead'. Sometimes it simply means the grave (Gen. 37:35) but other times it means the place where departed spirits go (Ps. 16:10). We believe that in the Old Testament period all the dead, good and evil, went to *sheol*, which was divided into two compartments (Luke 16:23). We believe also that at his resurrection Jesus brought the Old Testament saints out of that place, and now the righteous go into the immediate presence of God (Phil. 1:23; 2 Cor. 5:8). This place, called Hades, is now the place of confinement for the wicked dead (Rev. 20:13: 'Death and Hades').

The other word for hell is *Gehenna*, and means the final lake of fire where the wicked will be sent bodily, after the souls and bodies are reunited. The word comes from 'the Valley of the Son of Hinnom' (2 Chron. 33:6), a continual burning rubbish heap outside Jerusalem, used at one time for pagan sacrifices of human beings. After the final judgement (Rev. 20:14), death and hell are cast into the lake of fire, the second death. Death here refers to the bodies of the wicked who come forth from the grave, unite with their souls which had been confined in Hades, and are sentenced to eternal hell.

2. *Hell is a place of eternal misery.* The final locale of the wicked is described in the Bible as a place of torment (Rev. 14:10-11), punishment (Matt. 25:46) and destruction (2 Thess. 1:9). That there is suffering and misery in hell is clear from the fact that some strong figures portray it, such as fire (Matt. 18:8), smoke (Rev. 14:11) and darkness (Matt. 8:12). There people weep and gnash their teeth (8:12).

Since there are physical as well as psychological consequences to sin, we would assume that the wicked will have physical misery. But the central idea of hell is separation from God, meaning that in that place none of the comforts of God's presence and grace will be felt. Thus hell is the second death, meaning separation from God (Rev. 21:8). To the wicked Jesus says, 'Depart from me, you cursed, into the everlasting fire prepared for the devil and his angels' (Matt. 25:41). In hell men will be cut off from the 'presence of the Lord' (2 Thess. 1:9).

Certain isolated texts are used by some cults to prove that hell is not for ever. But the same word is used for this as for heaven (Matt. 25:46). In Mark 9:43-48, Jesus said five times that in hell the fire shall never be quenched. This indicates not only perpetual misery, but *conscious* misery. The unsaved will retain their memory (see Luke 16:27). Hopelessness will eat away at their spirit.

3. *Hell will be the just deserts of men because of their sin.* The second death is the 'wages' of sin, thus it is something which men earn (Rom. 6:23). It is the soul that *sins* that must die (Ezek. 18:4). The purpose for man's eternal abode, outside of Christ, is not for his betterment or reformation. Hell

is vindication of God's law, thus it will manifest the 'wrath' and righteous judgement of God (Rom. 2:5). God's law demands punishment for offenders. When law-breakers are not punished then law becomes mere advice. Only eternal separation from God is adequate payment for man's rebellion against his gracious Creator.

Since sinners will get their 'just deserts' there will no doubt be degrees of punishment in hell. In Luke 12:47-48 we read, 'And that servant who knew his master's will, and did not prepare himself or do according to his will, shall be beaten with many stripes. But he who did not know, yet committed things deserving of stripes, shall be beaten with few.' Punishment will be based on the number of sins, the quality of sins and the degree of light. Notice in this passage how knowledge enters into the picture. In Hebrews 10:29 we read of 'worse punishment', which those who sin against a gospel profession will experience.

4. *Hell explained.* The doctrine of endless punishment gives a reminder of two things that help to explain it.

a. *The free agency of man.* The wicked choose to rebel against God and thus choose hell. In a sense they get what they want. The natural man wants to be away from God; this is what he gets.

b. *The heinousness of sin.* We should never take sin lightly. God didn't. He sent his Son to pay the penalty for it on Calvary's cross. It cost God the supreme sacrifice. Those who deny the fact of eternal punishment as a rule take a light or casual attitude towards sin. If we have adequate concepts of the holiness of God we will not dispute the biblical doctrine of hell. Dreadful as it is, the truth of a conscious, eternal burning hell completes the scheme of salvation taught in the Bible, makes the grace of God stand out in more glorious colours, and enhances the gratitude of those who are redeemed.

Conclusion

The Bible contains a complete revelation from God to man about all the important matters that relate to God's character and man's salvation. The origin of the universe, the origin and character of man, sin, God's programme for man's recovery known as redemption, and the destiny of the universe are all explained so that no one should remain in ignorance. It is the glorious and pressing business of the church to proclaim this message to a world that needs it. May we who believe rejoice that God has shown his purposes to us and given us the privilege of sharing it.

Notes

1. Carl Sagan, from the television series *Cosmos*.
2. A. H. Strong, *Systematic Theology*, vol.1, Philadelphia: Judson Press, 1907, p.304.
3. Arthur Beiser ed., *The Earth*, Life Nature Library, New York: Time Incorporated, 1962, p.36.
4. Sir Bernard Lovell, 'The Origin and Evolution of the Universe', *The New Treasury of Science*, New York: Harper and Row, 1965, p.140.
5. Benjamin B. Warfield, *The Inspiration and Authority of the Bible*, Philadelphia: The Presbyterian and Reformed Publishing Company, 1948, p.133.
6. Arthur W. Pink, *The Inspiration of the Scriptures*, Swengel, Pennsylvania: Bible Truth Depot, 1917, pp.86-7.
7. John Wesley, *The Works of John Wesley*, 14 vols, London: Wesley Conference Office, 1872; reprint ed., Grand Rapids, Michigan: Zondervan Publishing House, n.d., vol.11, p.484.
8. Arthur W. Pink, *The Seven Sayings of the Saviour on the Cross*, Swengel, Pennsylvania: Bible Truth Depot, 1951, pp.114.
9. John Brown D.D., *Discourses and Sayings of Our Lord Jesus Christ, Illustrated in a Series of Expositions*, 3 vols, Edinburgh: William Oliphant and Sons, 1850, vol. 1, p.91.
10. Charles Hodge, *A Commentary on the Epistle to the Ephesians*, Grand Rapids, Michigan: Wm B. Eerdmans Publishing Company, 1954, p.225.
11. Louis Berkhof, *Systematic Theology*, Grand Rapids, Michigan: Wm B. Eerdmans Publishing Company, 1953, p.737.
12. Alvah Hovey, D.D. LL.D., *Manual of Systematic Theology and Christian Ethics*, Philadelphia: American Baptist Publication Society, 1877, p.364.

Index

Abel, 98-9

Abraham, 138, 162

Adam
  all men sinned in, 67-8
  fall of, 65-72
  object of God's attention and
    favour, 57
  original holiness of, 64
  placed under God's law, 62-3
  position in the original crea-
    tion, 61-2
  representative man, 65
  responsibility of, 61, 62-3
  sin imputed to the human
    race, 67-8
  sinful nature communicated
    to human race, 66-7

Adoption
  difference from civil adop-
    tion, 103-4
  results of, 104

Afflictions, 130

Age-day theory of creation,
  27

A-millennialism, 176

Anderson, Sir Robert, 168

Angels
  characteristics of, 28
  evil angels, 29-30
  holy angels, 30
  in the final judgement, 180
  number of, 28
  organization of, 28
  origin of, 28

Antichrist
  destroyed at Second Coming,
    166, 172
  makes war with saints, 169-
    70
  same as the 'man of sin', 166,
    169

Apostolic office
  temporary nature of, 145-6
  uniqueness of, 147-8

Atheism, 14, 17

Atonement
  God's acceptance of, 90
  special reference to the elect,
    87-8
  universal sufficiency of,
    87-8

Babylon, 29, 53-4

Scripture index

A wide range of excellent books on spiritual subjects is available from Evangelical Press. Please write to us for your free catalogue or contact us by e-mail.

Evangelical Press
Faverdale North Industrial Estate, Darlington, DL3 0PH, England

Evangelical Press USA
P. O. Box 825, Webster, New York 14580, USA

e-mail: sales@evangelicalpress.org
web: www.evangelicalpress.org